THE TRUTH ABOUT PARENTING

A UNIVERSAL MANUAL FOR PARENTING

H. JEAN 'STAR' GRAY

WESTBOW®
PRESS
A DIVISION OF THOMAS NELSON
& ZONDERVAN

WestBow Press books may be ordered through booksellers or by contacting:

WestBow Press
A Division of Thomas Nelson & Zondervan
1663 Liberty Drive
Bloomington, IN 47403
www.westbowpress.com
1 (866) 928-1240

ISBN: 978-1-4908-8103-4 (sc)
ISBN: 978-1-4908-8104-1 (e)

Library of Congress Control Number: 2015907935

Print information available on the last page.

WestBow Press rev. date: 05/19/2015

DEDICATION

This book is dedicated to my four children: LaShun, Leslie, Rodney, and Veronica. They have been an asset and an inspiration to me their entire lives, and they keep meaning in my life. My children have inspired and encouraged me through life's awesome journey. They never stop thanking me for being their mother (Mama to them). If I never told them before, I would like to tell them now. Thank you. Thank you for thanking me when you didn't have to. I thank God, and I will never stop thanking Him for giving me the opportunity to be your mama. I would also like to thank my late father and mother who gave me life. My parents always stayed focused, aimed high, and prayed.

Like everyone else in the world, I have my own story. Someday I will tell the world my story. For now, I want to tell you where I am in life. I wrote this book because I've learned a great deal through living who I am spiritually and even who and why I am as a person.

I give God all the praise for my life and for providing me with the wisdom I have attained.

Early on in my life there was an old woman who used to tell me, "I came up on the rough side of the mountain, and if'n ya wanna make it in life, ya got to thresh out ya row." I'm not at the end of my row yet, but I'm still thrashing. Thank you, Big Ma! The book of Proverbs is one way of telling the world, "Ya got to thresh out ya row!"

By H. Jean Gray

CONTENTS

INTRODUCTION

Books have been written on parenthood and child rearing; many are from a secular perspective, and some are from a spiritual perspective. This book, *The Truth about Parenting*, is designed to teach young adults how to be parents before they actually take on that role. It is written from a Christian, biblical perspective, and it embraces the principles set forth in the books of Proverbs and Ephesians.

There is no parenting manual that will teach people how to be parents. Contrary to popular opinion, there has been one since the beginning of time—the Holy Bible. We must accept that fact. The book of Proverbs in the Holy Bible is one of the most profound guides to personal living. It teaches us the principles of parental functioning. There is much more to learn from all sixty-five other books of the Bible, so don't discard or dismiss all others. Second Timothy 2:15 admonishes us to "study to show thyself approved unto God, a workman that needeth not to be ashamed, rightly dividing the word of truth."

In my book, *The Truth about Parenting*, you will find the simple facts on just how easy it is to become a well-rounded parent.

We can hear the cries of babies all over the world, asking the human race (us) to save them. They are crying for us to take our positions as positive parents and lead them to a safe haven and a sane world to live in.

I hear babies crying!

Chapter 1

Start Early

"Seek ye first the Kingdom of God and His righteousness, and all else will come" (Matt. 6:33).

Important! Don't be alarmed by the fact that some information in this book is intentionally repeated.

Start Early

The first step in learning to be a parent is learning to be a person. The first step in learning to be a person is learning to like yourself. The second step is learning to love yourself. Then you must discover who you really are. Acknowledging *whose* you are is one of the major steps to becoming a positive parent.

Q: Star, what makes you think I don't know who I am?

A: Most of us never stop to think about who we are. When you become acquainted with who you are, you can acknowledge *whose* you are. Accepting that you're a child of God, you take a major step toward becoming a positive parent.

In your quest to learn your true self, ask yourself these questions:

1. Do I really like myself?
2. What do I like about myself?
3. Why was I born?
4. Do I know everything there is to know or should know about myself?
5. Am I all I can be as a person?
6. What do I want to do with my life?
7. Where am I in my life right now?
8. Where do I go from here?
9. What do I want from the world, and what can I contribute to the world?
10. How do I prepare myself to get to where I want to go?
11. Can what I am doing now help me get to where I want to go with my life?
12. Am I doing what God has commanded me to do?

Teens need to know what is important, they want proper information

There are thousands of teenage parents! We must help our teenage children understand the proper time to become parents and what it means to be parents. Once you've gotten to know yourself, ask yourself whether you're ready for parenting. Am I prepared?

Potential parents, please try to complete your education before you take on the role of parenthood. Fulfilling such a role takes your full attention. Modern society supports the idea of single parenthood and other arrangements, but from the beginning, God ordained marriage between a husband and a wife (mother and father) before they multiplied themselves.

The reason why the first twenty-one years of age are considered so important is that at age twenty-one, an individual is legally an adult. In addition, this age allows a person time to finish the first stage of his or her secondary education. You see, education not only prepares you to work; it also helps to provide you with reasoning skills for life.

Reality check

The only way you can learn to like and/or love someone else is to learn to love or like yourself. There are too many people in the world who don't like themselves. To be a proper parent, you must love God, love yourself, love your spouse, and be willing to love your children. Get in touch with what you like about yourself, discover what your spouse loves about you, and love everything about your baby—he or she is a gift from God for only the two of you.

When you make it a point to be all you can be, it's easy to give all you have and all the child needs. That way, the dad and mom can concentrate on growing a happy, well-functioning family.

In today's society, a two-income family is the norm, and couples don't feel they can make it otherwise. But when a husband tells his wife she *must* go to work, he isn't providing for his family. A child needs his or her mother at home. A man needs his wife at home. A woman has to be at home to be a homemaker. Having a big house, a fancy car, and designer clothing is a dream of most people, but because of these material things, families are losing their children. Please stop saying, "I don't know what's wrong with my children" or "Lord, what is wrong with these children today?"

Being a provider is a big job, being a homemaker is a huge job, and being parents is a gigantic job. Talk about being together for a lifetime. Wow! Can you hear me now?

Q: Star, what do you mean when you say we're losing our children?

A: Look around you, parents. Your children don't respect you, themselves, or anyone else. Children are dropping out of school at an alarming rate; unwanted teenage pregnancy is out of control, and we're losing count of the number of unwanted children in the world or in the system. Whichever way you want to say it, children are turning to their peers for advice. A latchkey kid is in a dangerous situation. All these situations are results of our poor parenting skills now and in the past.

When we use the tools the Lord gave us to rear our children, then we can say, "Lord, thank You for the wonderful children you gave us." Our plans cannot work, because Jesus didn't give a command to succeed at our own plans. He only gave us a choice to do His will or not do His will. When you don't do His will, you aren't under His shield. Ephesians 6:11–18 admonishes us to

> put on the whole armor of God, that ye may
> be able to stand against the wiles of the devil.

12 For we wrestle not against flesh and blood but against principalities, against powers, against the rulers of the darkness of this world, against spiritual wickedness in high places. 13 Wherefore take unto you the whole armor of God that ye may be able to withstand in the evil days, and having done all, to stand. 14 Stand therefore, having your loins girt about with truth, and having on the breastplate of righteousness;15 And your feet shod with the preparation of the gospel of peace; 16 Above all, take the shield of faith, wherewith ye shall be able to quench all the fiery darts of the wicked. 17 And take the helmet of salvation, and the sword of the spirit, which is the word of God; 18 Praying always with prayer and supplication in the spirit, and watching thereunto with all perseverance and supplication for all saints.

Once we put on the the whole armor, build a proper relationship with your children

Some people say we cannot be our children's friends. The truth is, we must be our children's friends. However, we cannot be their pals. Please don't take these two words and make them say what you want them to say. A pal is someone your children hang out with, go to school with, and play with. A true friend will be with you to the end, talk to you even when he or she is angry with you, and help you see the light even in darkness (hint, parents).

Teach your children how to make choices. Don't let them just do whatever they want whenever they want. Children want you to give them positive directions. Children want to be guided to do what's correct. They want to respect others as well as to be respected. Parents, please, we must not ask our children to "do as I say and don't do what you see me do." Be the person your child can respect. Stop cursing around your children and do your best not to knowingly lie to them. Try very hard to leave them with people who won't hurt them. These days we cannot be too careful. Do things to include the entire family as often as possible.

If you're a drunkard, your child is more likely to drink. Proverbs 20:7 says, "The just man walketh in his integrity; his children are blessed after him." If you're a smoker, your child will often smoke, too. If you're always in jail, you're leaving a trail. If your hygiene is poor, your child will pick up on the same habit.

Proverbs 20:15 says that "wine is a mocker, strong drink is raging; and whosoever is deceived thereby isn't wise."

CHAPTER 2

MAN

God has appointed man as head over the entire world (Gen. 1:26). Then God said, "Let us [God and His Son Jesus Christ] make man in Our image, according to Our likeness, and let them rule over the fish of the sea and over the birds of the sky and over the cattle and over all the earth, and over every creeping thing that creeps on earth."

You cannot do this all by yourself

"Trust in the Lord with all thine heart; Lean not on thy own understanding. In all thy ways acknowledge Him, and He shall direct thy paths" (Prov. 3:5–6).

Man, God expects you to set a positive path for everything that goes on in this world. "And Jesus came and spoke to them saying, 'All authority has been given to me in heaven and on earth. Go there and make disciples of all nations, baptizing them in the name of the Father and of the Son and of the Holy Spirit, Teaching them to observe all things that I have commanded you; and lo, I am with you always, even to the end of the world. Amen'" (Matt. 28:18–20). Men, God will never leave you alone. Just pray and ask Him to help you in whatever you do. If you have a problem praying, use the example of the Lord's Prayer found in Matthew 6 (see appendix).

Here's an example: "Dear heavenly Father, I praise Your holy name! Thank You for Your grace and mercy, Your perfect gifts from heaven. I'm down here on this earth, coming before You as humble as I know how. I need You, Father, to show me how to do the things You will have me to do. I want to be a righteous man, a good man, a leader, father and a proper husband. Please show me where to go to learn how to be these things according to Your Word!"

Prayer isn't just words. It's also a righteous state of mind. You must read the Word to know what it says. You must believe!

Be sure that you've prepared yourself with the career you can be happy with. That way you're happy with yourself. Now it's easy for you to plan to provide for a family.

Ask yourself these questions:

1. Am I the man God would have me to be? Proverbs 26:16 says, "For a just *man* falleth seven times, and riseth up again: but the wicked shall fall into mischief."
2. Am I a real man? Proverbs 27:20 says, "Hell and destruction are never full; so the eyes of man are never satisfied." Proverbs 28:5 says, "Evil men understand not judgment: but they that seek the Lord understand all *things*."
3. If all men in the world were like me, what kind of world would this be?
4. Am I a leader?
5. Am I dependable?
6. How many men in the world are better at being a man than I am?

Important, reading these verses in Proverbs gives us an understanding of what is expected of us

Read the following (see appendix for cross references):

Proverbs 1:7 says, "The fear of the LORD *is* the beginning of knowledge: *but* fools despise wisdom and instruction."

Proverbs 4:5–9 says, "Get wisdom, get understanding; forget *it* not; neither decline from the words of my mouth. Forsake her not, and she shall preserve thee: love her, and she shall keep thee. Exalt her, and she shall promote thee: she shall bring thee to honour, when thou dost embrace her. She shall give to thine head an ornament of grace: a crown of glory shall she deliver to thee."

Proverbs 6:16–19 says, "These six *things* doth the Lord hate: yea, seven *are* an abomination unto him: A proud look, a lying tongue, and hands that shed innocent blood. An heart that deviseth wicked imaginations, feet that be swift in running to mischief. A false witness *that* speaketh lies, and he that soweth discord among brethren."

Proverbs 12:2 says, "A good *man* obtaineth favour of the Lord: but a man of wicked devices will he condemn."

Proverbs 14:12 says, "There is a way which seemeth right unto a man, but the end thereof *are* the ways of death."

Proverbs 15:19, 21, 32 says, "The way of the slothful *man is* as an hedge of thorns: but the way of the righteous *is* made plain … Folly *is* joy to *him that is* destitute of wisdom: but a man of understanding walketh uprightly … He that refuseth instruction despiseth his own soul: but he that heareth reproof getteth understanding."

Proverbs 16:2, 7–8, 18, 25 says, "All the ways of a man *are* clean in his own eyes; but the Lord weigheth the spirits … When a man's ways please the Lord, he maketh even his enemies to be at peace with him. Better *is* a little with righteousness than great revenues without right … Pride *goeth* before destruction, and an haughty spirit before a fall … There is a way that seemeth right unto a man, but the end thereof *are* the ways of death."

Proverbs 25:18–19 says, "A man that beareth false witness against his neighbor *is* a maul, and a sword, and a sharp arrow. Confidence in an unfaithful man in time of trouble *is like* a broken tooth, and a foot out of joint."

Proverbs 26:14 says, "*As* the door turneth upon his hinges, so *doth* the slothful upon his bed."

Proverbs 27:20 says, "Hell and destruction are never full; so the eyes of man are never satisfied."

Proverbs 28:5–6, 13, 21 says, "Evil men understand not judgment: but they that seek the Lord understand all *things* … He that covereth his sins shall not prosper:

but whoso confesseth and forsaketh *them* shall have mercy … To have respect of persons *isn't* good: but for a piece of bread *that* man will transgress."

Proverbs 29:25 says, "The fear of man bringeth a snare: but whoso putteth his trust in the Lord shall be safe."

Proverbs 30:9 says, "Lest I be full, and deny *thee*, and say, Who *is* the Lord? or lest I be poor, and steal, and take the name of my God *in vain*."

Proverbs 18:24 says, "A man *that hath* friends must shew himself friendly: and there is a friend *that* sticketh closer than a brother."

Proverbs 20:1, 4, 6, 24 says, "Wine *is* a mocker, strong drink *is* raging: and whosoever is deceived thereby isn't wise … The sluggard won't plow by reason of the cold; *therefore* shall he beg in harvest, and *have nothing* … Most men will proclaim everyone his own goodness: but a faithful man who can find? … Man's goings *are* of the Lord; how can a man then understand his own way?"

Proverbs 21:2, 8, 25 says, "Every way of a man *is* right in his own eyes: but the Lord pondereth the hearts … The way of man *is* froward and strange: but *as for* the pure, his work *is* right ... The desire of the slothful killeth him; for his hands refuse to labour."

Proverbs 22:24 says, "Make no friendship with an angry man; and with a furious man thou shalt not go."

HUSBAND

Proverbs 18:22 says, "Whoso findeth a wife findeth a good thing, and obtaineth favor of the Lord." Once you become a husband, this is one more time to pray. We as humans cannot do this alone.

Here's an example of a prayer:

Dear Father,

Wonderful, merciful, all-knowing, and gracious Father, I come before You today as an empty vessel before a full fountain, begging for Your mercy! First, Master, please forgive me for all of my sins. You have given me two of the most powerful jobs in the world, and I thank You for them both. You made me ruler over all things in this world, and You gave me a wife to love. Please give me the strength and the desire to learn how to be the man You will have me be in both of these positions. You told me in Your Word that You would fight my battles, so here I am, Lord. I'm ready for the battlefield. Please lead me; I am ready to follow. In addition, Father, if I am not asking amiss, please allow me to be a father. My wife and I are ready to become parents in two years, if that is Your will. Please give me the strength to stay in Your Word and be the leader, the husband, and the father You will have me to be, that You commanded me to be. Father, I want to be like You.

Here are some important facts and questions to ask yourself.

- Love your wife (Eph. 5:25). "Husbands, love your wives, even as Christ also loved the church, and gave himself for it."
- Can my wife submit to the kind of leadership I am demonstrating? Proverbs 27:8 says, "As a bird that wandereth from her nest, so *is* a man that wandereth from his place."
- Would I have wanted my dad to be the kind of husband I am?
- I must be the best husband I can be.
- Husbands, once you enter into marriage, remaining friends with other women or making new friendships with women isn't a wise idea. Such relationships can create issues of loyalty and trust, and bring about jealousy and dissention.

1. Husbands, don't ever stop courting your wife.
2. A happy man and woman make great parents.

3. Husbands, keep your birth family out of your business—marriage is between a husband and wife.

4. Please be the head of your house or family, teaching your children by example. Proverbs 11:29 says, "He that troubleth his own house inherits the wind: and the fool shall be servant to the wise at heart."

FATHER

Father, please allow your one wife to be the mother of all the children you're going to have. Having all your children by one wife and under one roof gives you a better chance of reaching all of them—wife and children.

Father, don't forget to tell your wife and daughters they are beautiful. This enhances their understanding of need for sense of self-worth. Open doors for your wife and daughters as you would for any other woman. The way you treat the women in your life helps them to know they are worthy. When your daughter seeks a husband, she will look for a man like you, whether good or bad. Father, play with your children and teach them rules to different games. Find out what your son wants to be when he grows up and teach him how to work in that direction. Sometime you may not know how to teach him these skills—learn and get some help. Always attend as many of your children's functions as possible. Both parents should take your children to PTSA (Parent, Teacher, Student Association) meetings. Attend the church Christ purchased with His blood (Eph. 4:5–6) as a family and teach your children how to live according to the Scriptures.

- Love your wife and children.
- Keep an open line of communication with your wife and children.

- Set and keep household rules for your family.
- Be a positive example for your son.
- Please don't let your son see you mistreat his mother.
- Take part in PTSA and know your child's school environment.
- A good practice for any family is to have regular family meetings.

Read Proverbs 20:7: "The just *man* walketh in his integrity: his children *are* blessed after him."

Read Proverbs 14:30: "A sound heart *is* the life of the flesh: but envy the rottenness of the bones."

Dad, a survey of one hundred boys revealed the following:

• Who would you like to take you to the barber shop?	Dad	100%
• Who would you like to be like when you grow up?	Dad	80%
• A sports personality		20%
• Who is your hero?	Dad	50%
• Name a superhero.	Dad	50%
• Do you know your dad?	Yes	75%
• Does your dad live with you?	Yes	45%

• I live with my stepfather.	30%
• I don't know my dad.	25%

Dads, we can fix this problem if we change our ways of doing things in life.

CHAPTER 3

WOMAN

Who can find a virtuous woman? For
her price is far above rubies.
—Proverbs 31:10

Ladies, we're in control of our lives before we get married. Please bring everything God gave you at birth to your marriage ceremony. This way on your wedding day you can feel like the most beautiful woman in the whole world. You're a diamond, even if you're still in the showcase, and you haven't yet been picked. You're still a diamond, so stay brilliant and keep on shining. Your day will come, and you will have everything.

Ask yourself the following:

- Am I the kind of woman God would have me to be?

- Why do I want to be a wife?
- Why do I want to be a mother?

Proverbs helps us to understand the answer to these questions

Important Read the following (see appendix cross reference to these verses):

Proverbs 14:33 says, "Wisdom resteth in the heart of him that hath understanding: but *that which is* in the midst of fools is made known."

Proverbs 15:33 says, "The fear of the Lord *is* the instruction of wisdom; and before honour *is* humility."

Proverbs 20:15 says, "There is gold, and a multitude of rubies: but the lips of knowledge *are* a precious jewel."

Proverbs 21:9 says, "*It is* better to dwell in a corner of the housetop, than with a brawling woman in a wide house."

Proverbs 22:24 says, "Make no friendship with an angry man; and with a furious man thou shalt not go."

Proverbs 31:30 says, "Favour is deceitful, and beauty is vain: but a woman that feareth the Lord, she shall be praised."

WIFE

Proverbs 31:11–31 (see appendix for a cross reference) says,

11The heart of her husband doth safely trust in her, so that he shall have no need of spoil. 12 She will do him good and not evil all the days of her life. 13 She seeketh wool, and flax, and worketh willingly with her hands. 14 She is like the merchants' ships; she bringeth her food from afar. 15 She riseth also while it is yet night, and giveth meat to her household, and a portion to her maidens. 16 She considereth a field, and buyeth it: with the fruit of her hands she planteth a vineyard. 17 She girdeth her loins with strength, and strengtheneth her arms. 18 She perceiveth that her merchandise is good: her candle goeth not out by night. 19 She layeth her hands to the spindle, and her hands hold the distaff. 20 She stretcheth out her hand to the poor; yea, she reacheth forth her hands to the needy. 21She is not afraid of the snow for her household: for all her household are clothed with scarlet. 22 She maketh herself coverings of tapestry; her clothing is silk and purple. 23 Her husband is known in the gates, when he sitteth among the elders of the land. 24 She maketh fine linen, and selleth it; and delivereth girdles unto the merchant. 25 Strength and honour are her clothing; and she shall rejoice in time to come.26 She openeth her mouth with wisdom; and in her tongue is the law of kindness. 27 She looketh well to the ways of her household, and eateth not the bread of idleness. 28 Her children arise up, and call her blessed; her husband also, and he praiseth her. 29Many daughters have done virtuously, but thou excellest them all. 30 Favour is deceitful, and beauty is vain: but a woman that feareth the Lord, she shall be praised. 31 Give her of the fruit of her hands; and let her own works praise her in the gates.

1. Not knowing how to cook isn't an option.
2. Am I a virtuous woman?
3. Should I be a submissive wife?
4. Is my husband proud to have me as a wife because I'm beautiful both inside and out?
5. Where can I go to find out how to be a real woman? (The book of Proverbs teaches you how to be a real woman, person, and wife.)
6. Did I learn from my mother's teachings and her mistakes?
7. Wife, keep your birth family out of your business between you and your husband.

8. Wife, it isn't wise to remain friends with males or to make new friends with males after you're married (this is a deal breaker).

Q: Should I be a submissive wife?

A: Ephesians 5:22 says, "Wives, submit yourselves unto your own husband, as unto the Lord."

MOTHER

This position is viewed as sacred. Real mothers are viewed as beacons of light who draw their rays from heaven.

The honor of being a mother is bestowed on us not because of the goodness of us as women but because of the unmerited grace of God.

Ask yourself these questions

1. Would I have wanted my mother to be the kind of mother I am?
2. If all the mothers in the world were like me, what kind of world would this be?
3. Mother, love your husband and your children.
4. Make sure you're in touch with the entire environment of our child's school.
5. Remember, cooking is an important part of family life. Not knowing how to cook isn't an option.
6. Cleanliness is next to godliness (keep your house and family clean).

CHAPTER 4

COUPLES

After you've prepared yourself to be the people God would have you to be, this is the time to pray for the wife or husband God has for you. Once you've identified that special person, make sure you're equally yoked. Being godly yoked means having something in common; both should be Christians in the church Jesus Christ shed His blood for. Both should have most of the same ideas about life. Learn each other's likes, dislikes, and wants. Make sure the playing field is level. Do you both want the same number of children? Understanding each other's roles in the relationship is very important.

This list of items are very important to agree on.

1. Faith
2. Knowing the type Food the two of you like is helpful

3. You may not think that colors or important but they are

4. Some of the things you both like to do

5. Talk about places you like to go this is good to know about each other

6. Entertainment helps with planning date night and vacations

7. Travel (where both have been and where you want to go later in life)

8. Talk about the types of friends you both want once you're married.

9. Make sure you share information about your past (no surprises later, please).

10. Always get to know each other's families (important).

11. Once you feel sure you want to get married, talk about how you're going to increase your family before you both agree to a plan (always have a plan B in whatever you do).

12. Remember, plans are just that—plans. Stick as closely to your plans as you possibly can, but plans do change.

13. Get spiritual counseling before you get married.

Q: Star, what does this have to do with parenting children?

A: If you aren't self-disciplined, how can you teach your children positive behavior?

MARRIAGE

Lovebirds, learning parenting doesn't start when you have children. You must condition yourselves to become positive parents.

The husband and wife are the only two people who can end a marriage. Anyone who enters that relationship will have to come through the man or woman, thus affecting the entire family. (The best parenting is done when both parents are in the home until death do they part.)

Read the following (appendix is a cross reference):

These verses from Proverbs are guides to help you understand why the above paragraph is important

Proverbs 3:5–6 says, "Trust in the Lord with all thine heart; and lean not unto thine own understanding. In all thy ways acknowledge him, and he shall direct thy paths."

Proverbs 4:5–9 says, "Get wisdom, get understanding: forget *it* not; neither decline from the words of my mouth. Forsake her not, and she shall preserve thee: love her, and she shall keep thee. Wisdom *is* the principal thing; *therefore* get wisdom: and with all thy getting get understanding. Exalt her, and she shall promote thee: she shall bring thee to honour, when thou dost embrace her. She shall give to thine head an ornament of grace: a crown of glory shall she deliver to thee."

Proverbs 6:16–19 says, "These six *things* doth the Lord hate: yea, seven *are* an abomination unto him: A proud look, a lying tongue, and hands that shed innocent blood, An heart that deviseth wicked imaginations, feet that be swift in running to mischief, A false witness *that* speaketh lies, and he that soweth discord among brethren."

Proverbs 9:10 says, "The fear of the Lord *is* the beginning of wisdom: and the knowledge of the holy *is* understanding."

Proverbs 18:21 says, "Death and life *are* in the power of the tongue: and they that love it shall eat the fruit thereof."

Proverbs 20:15 says, "There is gold, and a multitude of rubies: but the lips of knowledge *are* a precious jewel."

Please don't live above one salary. If two incomes are what you must have, use the second salary to do something other than pay bills.

Here are things you want to start with in your marriage:

1. Jesus Christ
2. Trust
3. Hope
4. Love
5. Like (disaster—being in love with someone you don't like)
6. Understanding (understand that hygiene is very important)

Read the following (see appendix The Proverbs Book From the Bible):

Proverbs 9:10 says, "The fear of the Lord *is* the beginning of wisdom: and the knowledge of the holy *is* understanding."

Proverbs 14:30, 33 says, "A sound heart *is* the life of the flesh: but envy the rottenness of the bones ... Wisdom resteth in the heart of him that hath understanding: but *that which is* in the midst of fools is made known."

Proverbs 15:2 says, "The tongue of the wise useth knowledge aright: but the mouth of fools poureth out foolishness."

Things you don't want in a real marriage:

1. A cheater
2. Being cash strapped
3. Misbehaving child/children
4. Bad advice (friends, family, neighbors, and so forth

See Appendix The book of Proverbs these verses can help to guide you in all walks of life Proverbs 12:19 says, "The lip of truth shall be established for ever: but a lying tongue *is* but for a moment."

Proverbs 20:11 says, "Even a child is known by his doings, whether his work *be* pure, and whether *it be* right."

If possible, don't enter into a marriage with the following:

1. Bills
2. Friends who don't mean you any good
3. A dependency (drugs, strong drink, secrets of any kind, and so forth)
4. A pregnancy (wait until after the wedding to get pregnant and have children)

Read the entire (Appendix) book of Proverbs a very tangible guide

Chapter 5

Parents

All the above pave the way to becoming informed people who are ready for positive parenting.

Parents, a child is a gift from God! Parenting can be viewed as the hardest and most important job in the whole world, although it can also be the easiest job in the whole world when this is what you want to do.

Parents, start early by talking to your children. Love them and teach them how to love you. When the proper time comes, have family meetings. Let the children help you make plans. When and if the plans change, tell them. Children understand more than you think they do. Be your children's true friend but not their pal. Listen to them. They don't want to be your pal. Talk *to* them, not *at* them. Please, parents, don't curse your children.

These verses are here to act as a guide/light for easy navigation.

James 3:8 says, "But the tongue can no man tame; it is an unruly evil, full of deadly poison." Talk to your children and teach them how to talk to you properly.

Proverbs 22:6 says, "Train up a child in the way he should go, and when he is old, he will not depart from it."

Proverbs 3:12 says, "For whom the Lord loveth, he correcteth; even as a father the son whom he delighteth."

Proverbs 13:24 says, "He that spareth his rod hateth his son, but he that loveth him chasteneth him betimes."

Proverbs 17:6 says, "Children's children are the crown of old men; and the glory of children are their fathers."

Proverbs 22:15 says, "Foolishness is bound in the heart of a child; but the rod of correction shall drive it far from him."

Proverbs 23:13–14 says, "Withhold not correction from the child: for thou beatest him with the rod, he shall not die. [*Rod* doesn't mean blunt trauma, large object! *Rod* here means belt, ruler, or paddle; age appropriate.] Thy shall beat him with the rod, and shalt deliver his soul from hell."

Proverbs 29:15 says, "The rod of reproof gives wisdom: but a child left to himself bringeth his mother to shame."

PREGNANCY

You have become a vessel through which God will deliver one of His perfect beings, and He left instructions for parents to teach the child to stay perfect until his or her death.

Mom, now is the time for you to pray a serious prayer. For example:

> Our Father who art in heaven, I praise Your holy name. Oh kind, gracious and merciful Father, please hear my cry! Lord, I am asking You to forgive me for all of my sins. I know that I haven't always obeyed Your commands. Give me the space and time to improve my understanding of You and my behavior. Father, You have given me an opportunity and the responsibilities to be a righteous woman, wife, and mother. I want to be all You want me to be. Please help me! Help me to be the kind of parent You would have me to be. Please give us a healthy baby. Also, help my husband and me to be in one mind in rearing our child to be like You!

You will need a proper diet and proper rest while you're pregnant. There is proper attire for a pregnant woman (no tight clothing). You look great and feel great when you're focused on what you're doing. You will have and get respect for yourself, your husband, and others; and your baby won't feel stressed from tight clothing while you're pregnant.

1. Do all you can to be happy while you're pregnant.
2. Get plenty of rest and sleep.
3. Don't use profanity—your baby can hear you.
4. Don't consume strong drink; it can cause birth defects.
5. Don't smoke; this can cause birth defects also.
6. Go for a walk every day. It is good to stay active in a healthy way.
7. Check with your doctor to ascertain how sexually active you should be while carrying your baby.
8. Don't ask the doctor to induce your labor because you're tired of carrying your baby. God put that baby there, and He can and will bring the baby into the world when it is time for you to deliver a healthy baby.

Much of this advice will help you to avoid low birth weight or children with mental and/or physical challenges for life.

NEWBORN/AFTER BIRTH

Always be happy with the gift God has given to you, whether a boy or girl.

*Make sure your home is conducive to rearing a baby or child. Keep a log on your children. Each child should have his or her own log (doctor's visits and other activities, such as dance, vocal, and music lessons).

Parents here is a list of important tips.

- Please don't allow your newborn to sleep with you. You can accidentally roll over on your child while you're asleep.
- Hug and kiss your children before you put them to bed every night.
- A safe crib is important.
- Make sure your child's room is close to your room so you will be able to hear your baby (you can use a baby monitor).
- Check when you hear a cry or cough.
- Sometimes a parent can feel whether something is wrong with the baby.
- If you wake up cold and have covers on you, check to see whether the baby has kicked his or her covers off and is cold.

- Check whether there are bugs in the crib.
- Check often to make sure a small object of any kind hasn't fallen into the crib.
- Sometimes a baby will vomit and not cry out, so do random checks to see whether he or she has been sleep for a while. A baby can choke on his or her own vomit.
- Don't wait for your child to cry to change him or her (check for a wet diaper).
- If your baby's skin looks red and raw, he or she possibly has a rash. A rash is painful. Clean the area with soap and water (not wipes). Apply Vaseline (or some type of medicated cream) to the affected area. This will help the area heal faster.
- Hold your baby during feedings.
- When your child is old enough to eat on his or her own, don't allow him or her to eat in the kitchen alone (he or she may choke on food or water).
- Holding your baby allows him or her to get to know you—your scent, color, and touch. This helps your baby to be cautious of strangers.
- Talk and sing to your baby and smile for him or her when you hold him or her. These actions teach your baby to feel loved and secure.

*When you pay close attention to your baby, you can learn what each cry means, and each time he or she cries, you will know how to respond. Is he or she wet or hungry? Does he or she just need to be held? Is he or she too hot, cold, or afraid?

- Baby learns your voice, language, words, and different sounds.
- Read to your child every day.
- Play music.
- Make sure your baby or child isn't overdressed for hot weather or underdressed for cold weather; this can make the baby ill.
- Leaving your baby or child alone in a room for long periods of time makes him or her feel afraid, if he or she is awake.
- Leaving children with people they don't know or don't like makes them very afraid.
- Leaving them with anyone for long periods makes them feel anxious, insecure, and afraid; and it can cause stomachaches, vomiting, and so forth.

Bulletin

These things will make your child sick, don't be the one to make your own child sick!

*** Things that are harmful to your child.

***Please don't give your child alcohol at any age.

***Secondhand smoke is harmful.

***Drugs are deadly.

SCHEDULE FOR FEEDING/BEDTIME

Wash your hands before you feed your baby. Be sure to use sterilized utensils at each feeding. Please don't talk on the telephone while trying to feed your baby.

Important: feed your baby age-appropriate food, balanced meals, and proper amounts. Limit sweet desserts, candies, sweet drinks, cookies, cereal, and so forth. Foods produced today contain many more additives than food in past years; many foods today cause obesity and can cause your baby or child to become ill if you aren't selective. (If there's any possible way you can plant a vegetable garden each summer, please do so. These foods are fresh and healthy for your baby and family.

Give your child breakfast every morning. This is very important once he or she starts school. A good diet is important (eggs, grits, oatmeal, milk and bread, water). Limit amounts of meat and juice. A hot meal and a hug from a parent are a good start for every day. Also, make sure children are taught to wash their hands before and after meals and each time they eat.

- Children should drink plenty of water every day.
- Try hard to have the family enjoy two meals together every day (if not two, at least one). If one, try to make it the dinner meal.

- Never allow your child to walk through the house while he or she is eating.
- Don't allow your child to drink from a container you or anyone else has drunk from, not even another child.
- Never allow children to eat a little bit, run around, and eat a little bit more.

NAP TIME

It is important that your child be on a schedule for naps and evening bedtime at age-appropriate times and all the way through secondary education.

Sample Schedules
- Bedtime, zero to five years   8:00 or 8:30 p.m.
- Nap time, zero to five years   11:30 a.m. or noon
- Bedtime, six to ten years   8:30 or 9:00 p.m.
- Eleven to fourteen years   9:00 or 9:30 p.m.
- Fifteen to eighteen years   10:30 or 11:00 p.m.

Eight hours of sleep are important every day (say prayers before getting into bed).

Proper sleep helps with behavior, learning, and proper growth.

Schedule time for bathing.

Important: schedule time for play and TV (know what your child is watching). All day long, there is hideous language being used on TV. The more your child hears positive words, the less likely he or she will use hideous words.

TODDLERS

- Talk to your children and hug them a lot at this age.
- Teach your child his or her real name.
- Teach your child how to spell his or her name.
- Show your child how to share.
- Children have to be taught not to lie (please demonstrate this behavior for them).
- Don't allow them to climb, since climbing for small children can be dangerous.
- Tell them the names of everything they wear or everything you give them to eat or play with.
- I know this task is asking a lot, but if you write the names of everything in your house and tape the name to each item, your child's vocabulary will grow very fast (from two years up).
- When you say no, mean it.
- Keep your children on schedule (for most things).
- Watch them closely; they need to be taught not to put things in their mouths.
- Teach them to tie their shoes.
- Clean their runny noses properly (place the tissue in a trash container, not on the floor or table).
- Teach them to use their words, not tears, to get what they want.

- Teach them to pick up their toys and put them back in the special place where they are kept.
- By the age of fifteen months, the child needs to be potty trained (children are going to school much earlier, so they need to be taught words like *urinate* and *defecate*, not *pee pee* or *boo boo* for the potty).
- Please take your baby outside most days, weather permitting. Going outside is an important part of growth and development. Don't leave him or her alone outside for even a second.
- Try hard *not* to be on the telephone while you're playing outside with your child.
- Please don't allow your child to hit or talk back at any age, even if he or she is playing.

Preschool/Kindergarten

Teach them the important things early.

- Don't talk to strangers.
- Don't leave this age alone anywhere (indoors or outdoors).
- Children under fourteen shouldn't be left in a car or at home alone.
- Don't send a child this age to school on a bus. If the child must ride the bus, take him or her to the bus and watch the child get on the bus. Make sure the school has a plan in place to get children of this age off the bus and to their classrooms. In addition, be there when your child returns home and get him or her off the bus every day.
- The child must know how to follow rules the teacher gives.
- Please teach your child that he or she must do what the teacher tells him or her to do.
- If your child feels that the teacher is in error, ask him or her to talk the matter over with you and allow you to help him or her understand or correct the problem (this rule should apply to anyone whom you trust your child with).
- Don't approach that teacher or adult when you're angry.

- Whenever you leave your child with anyone, question your child about what went on.
- If you've been away from your child for any length of time and he or she seems to feel or act in an unusual manner, find out why.
- Make sure your child understands that he or she must follow your rules. Expect good behavior at all times.
- Don't let your child tear up your house or anyone's home. Explain to the child that he or she isn't allowed to touch things unless he or she is asked to do so. Don't let your child walk around in other people's homes unless he or she has permission to do so.
- At church please sit in the area that is designated for people with children. Start early teaching your children to sit down at all times in church. Take them to the restroom before the service begins. When or if they get restless, please take them out. One way to keep children quiet is to bring a toy that won't make a sound. A toddler can write on paper—no crayons, please, but colored pencils will work. Hope and pray that the child goes to sleep.
- Most churches have a nursery with a viewing screen to see and hear the sermon.
- Teach your child the proper behavior wherever you are.

ELEMENTARY-AGE CHILDREN

Organizing your community is part of parenting. Allowing elementary-age children to play freely and unsupervised in the neighborhood in groups can mean trouble. We all have different parenting skills in many ways. We must organize our neighborhoods. We must organize planned activities for our children. This is one way to teach our children how to behave in a school environment and in the real world. When we begin to develop strong families and strong neighborhoods, we will begin to see strong churches and a sane world for us to live in. Children want to be told the right things to do. However, you must start at birth. Don't wait until they are out of control. It's too late at that point.

Parents, schools must have dress codes. If these codes aren't in place, it is the parents' responsibility to see that the school puts them in place. When we teach our children to dress properly at an early age, they will more likely wear proper attire when they become adults.

Important Focal Points (flashing light)

- Don't allow your child to tell you what he or she doesn't want to do.
- Parents, set the rules in your home and demand that the children follow them.

- Ask your child whether he or she had a nice day at school.

- Homework should be done daily. Most teachers have a homework folder that is sent home daily (parents, ask the teacher or child about this folder).

- If your child isn't bringing homework home, check with the teacher.

- If for some reason you cannot help your child with his or her homework, ask the teacher to allow your child to stay after school for individual help.

- When your child needs to stay after school, please give him or her a snack. Hunger won't allow the child to focus. In addition, pick the child up at the exact time that is agreed upon.

- Check your child's book bag daily for announcements.

- Set positive rules and allow your lifestyle to demonstrate for your children how these rules are to be followed.

- Don't keep your child out of school because you or the child is sleepy.

- Try hard to be sure children are in school every day.

- When your child becomes twelve, teach him or her the scientific name and proper function of his or her body parts.

- This is the time to tell your child the truth about sex. Be sure to explain that God designed sex only for married people.
- The more a child knows the real truth about sex, the less he or she will engage in it.
- This age-group doesn't need any of the multimode communication technology that is available, period.
- Parents, don't give your child alcohol at any age or any time.
- Parents, please don't allow a brother or sister in this age-group to share a bed or room together (past four years of age).

GIRLS

- Parents, the less makeup and grown-up clothing our little girls wear, the younger they will look. The more grown-up things she wears, the more she will attract unwanted male attention, even at this age.
- Twelve years old is soon enough to allow your little girl to wear lip gloss or nail polish.
- Fifteen is old enough for high-heel shoes and makeup.
- Please don't allow your little girl to wear pants or blue jeans every day.
- Teach girls to wear dresses (age appropriate) and demonstrate how they should sit (never sit so that anyone can see under the dress past the knees).
- Playing with their friends at school and outside after school is plenty enough talk time. This age-group shouldn't be allowed to spend much time on the telephone.
- Parents, please don't allow your elementary-age child to own a cell phone or carry one.
- Teach your elementary-age girls that pursuing boys at any age is inappropriate.
- Twelve-year-old girls need to know everything there is to know about their monthly (menstrual) cycle. Show them what they need.

- Give them a little care package to take to school and explain that this isn't something they share. This is personal.
- Explain how to care for themselves at school or anywhere away from home.
- Teach them how to refresh themselves during the day.
- Sanitary pads in any shape or size shouldn't be placed in a toilet. They should be properly wrapped and disposed of in a waste receptacle.

BOYS

- Children at any age or sex shouldn't be allowed to carry a weapon.
- Parents, teach your boys to use proper language when talking to a female, even if she isn't acting like a lady.
- It is also very important for boys to wear proper attire.
- Underwear is just that, to be worn under the clothing.
- Parents, we must make time to steer our children in a positive direction.
- Parents, you're your child's first teacher.
- Engage your child in sports (his own interest). Sports can help with discipline.
- If there is a Boy Scouts troop in your area, get your son involved.
- Help your sons to balance their schedules with sports and academics (they need both for balanced growth).
- If not sports, help them to develop any talent they may have. It is very important.

SIMPLE ACHES OR PAINS

Sometimes children may tell you they are ill just so they can get your attention. Give them your attention.

Child—When a child tells you that his or her stomach hurts ...

Parent—Ask whether he or she needs to go to the bathroom. (Sometimes a child can have gas in the stomach.) Accompany the child to the bathroom and check the color of the bowel movement. Talk with your pediatrician about the color and its importance. Sometimes a child will hold their stool to avoid the restroom for whatever reason. Maybe ask them if they would like for you to go to the restroom with them, this will help with some of their stomach-aches.

Child—When your child tells you he or she has a headache ...

Parent—Maybe he or she is just sleepy or hungry or just needs attention. Pay close attention to be sure.

Child—When your child tells you he or she is hot,

Parent -----make sure the child isn't overdressed. Then check his or her temperature. If it is above 102 degrees, give the child some chilled water or wipe him or her down with a cool towel, put him or her down to rest, and keep checking on him or her.

Parent—Ask the pharmacist to help you with home remedies to help your child feel better. This measure will prevent unnecessary visits to the doctor's office.

HIGH SCHOOL CHILDREN

- Parents, these people are still children, no matter the sex, color, race, culture, nationality, social status, economic status, size, academic ability, or geographical location.
- Sex isn't a recreational sport. It isn't designed for unmarried people at any age.
- We're in error when we give our children permission and provide a place for them to engage in sex.
- Sex is one of the most deadly weapons ever processed when it is used in an improper manner. Recreational sex kills and causes people to become homeless, jobless, dreadfully ill, blind, and crippled; it can cause children to be born unwanted and unloved. It can cause divorce. It can cause people to be deported, motherless, fatherless, sent to jail, and so forth.
- High school is the age when the epidemic begins, and children are starting younger each year.
- Sex is a chosen enemy.
- Father, please don't teach your boys that having sex makes them men.
- Contrary to popular opinion, sex is a private act between married couples behind closed doors.
- There are many ways to keep this age-group busy.

YOUNG WOMEN

Here's a list of activities teenagers can become involved in that are much more productive than sex:

1. Sewing
2. Cooking/baking
3. Going to charm school
4. Knitting/doing macramé or embroidery
5. Hair styling
6. Doing nails
7. Makeup
8. sports
9. Quilting
10. Babysitting
11. House cleaning
12. Working with computers
13. Doing crafts
14. Being involved a book club
15. Writing
16. Taking voice lessons
17. Taking music lessons
18. Canning foods
19. Freezing foods

YOUNG MEN

Here's a list of activities teenagers can become involved in that are much more productive than sex:

1. Playing sports
2. Doing ROTC
3. Landscaping
4. Barbering
5. Detailing a car
6. Being a chef
7. Writing
8. Taking voice lessons
9. Taking music lessons
10. Gardening

All these suggestions can also be used to build careers starting in college.

FRIENDS

Be selective about who your children's friends are. This era won't allow us to let our children spend the night in each other's homes. It isn't advisable.

CHAPTER 6

RESPONSIBLE PARENTING

Parenting is the hardest but most rewarding job you'll ever have. I want to get right to the point. What is so hard about parenting? Performing the duties of a parent isn't hard. The only thing we must do is follow the divine plan God has given us. What makes the job easy is wanting to do the job properly.

To make sure the job is easy, use the plan God gave us to prepare ourselves to become willing persons. We're good by our own standards; however, we aren't the meter by which we will be measured. The reason the world wasn't designed the way we wanted it to be is because we would have all killed each other by now. God wouldn't allow all of us to kill each other. Each day He gives us a new chance to get it right.

Now let's follow the simple steps at the beginning of the book, which are just common sense to parenting our children.

We must treat our children properly. Parents and adults are doing the evil, hideous things that are being done to our children. Many of us became very angry when the law was written telling us we couldn't use corporal punishment on our children. Let me explain the contents of that law. Some of us aren't just spanking our children; we're criminally abusing them. Children were going to emergency rooms with repeated broken bones and concussions; they'd been raped for years or were malnourished, dehydrated, or burned. They had missing limbs, or they'd been left alone in the house for weeks, and the list goes on.

Judges in the courts knew that if they allowed these crimes to continue happening to our children at such an alarming rate, the justice system would have been accused of not protecting our children. Therefore, the law in most states made it illegal to hit a child in any fashion.

These children's own parents, close friends, or family members committed these crimes. Because of this law, we make it say what we want it to say. We use this law to justify our poor parenting skills and unruly children.

Nonetheless, my friends, what we're doing in this day and age is simply a form of poor parenting. People, if we don't fix ourselves, it isn't humanly possible to ever measure up to becoming proper parents.

Let me assure you that the way you treat your children today will make a direct effect on their lives in the future. Parents, all the law is asking us to do is stop committing criminal acts against your children or anyone else's children. In addition, we aren't teaching our teenage children the proper way to be responsible for younger children. Please don't allow teenage children to babysit your younger children or anyone else's child.

WHAT PROPER PARENTING STOPS

1. Sin in any form (child abuse)
2. Shacking up
3. Domestic violence (battered wives)
4. Bullying
5. Bad manners
6. Negative behavior
7. Children telling lies
8. Stealing or robbing in any form on all levels
9. Runaways
10. Teen pregnancy
11. Children taking part in gangs
12. The opportunities for strangers to get children's attention
13. Negative Internet interaction
14. Blatant disrespect for self and others
15. Dangerous behaviors
16. Teen deaths (speeding cars, drugs, sex, guns, and knives)
17. The use of any kind of technological device while operating a motor vehicle
18. School dropouts
19. The sale and use of drugs
20. Battered children
21. Child molestation
22. Murder

WHAT PROPER PARENTING IMPROVES

1. Education
2. Human behavior (from childhood through adulthood) in people in neighborhoods, churches, cities, counties, states, countries, and the world's families
3. Divorce rates
4. Unwanted pregnancies (**unwed pregnancies at any age**)
5. Positive involvement in neighborhood organizations!!!

WIDOWED PARENTS

Sometimes the death of a spouse forces someone to be in a single-parent position. This is a hard place to be. Prayerfully, this won't happen to very many families. We must always keep in mind that these situations can happen. Plan for your future. Every family in the world needs insurance, no matter their situation.

Take a long hard look at important decisions and the fact that they affects the entire family (Tips)

- Dad, Mom, don't be so quick to remarry.
- Don't bring one person after another (strangers) into your home interacting with your children.
- Don't give your children to your parents or to anyone else to care for them. You're the person they want and need. If living with a parent or another family member is what you must do, try to do most of the caring for your own children. Teach them how to clean up behind themselves and help with the chores. Teach them the difference between living in someone else's home and living in their own place. Help them to understand how to ask for what they want or need. When children understand shared living, this will help to make them well-rounded persons. This will prevent

you from having to move around a lot. A stable place to live helps to make adults and children happy.

- If at all possible, wait until children are grown up to the point that they can understand a little better when you decide you're going to get married again.
- Please get counseling for them; it is so important.
- If you marry again and both spouses have underage children, please get counseling. Blending a family isn't always as simple as you may think.
- There is help for a solo parent, and there are programs designed for single parents. Some of these programs are presented through churches and other social agencies. Do everything you can to help your children be all they can be, no matter how hard it is. Your effort will pay off in the end.

SINGLE PARENTS

Please follow chapters 1–4. However, this manual is written to discourage single parents. The New Testament teaches us that premarital sex is disobeying God. When we obey God, there will be no premarital sex and therefore no single parents, except in cases of death or divorce.

Q: Star, is your advice on parenting or on marriage?

A: Parenting is my main goal here, however a happy, health and spiritual marriage is a safe environment for parenting.

PARENTS

This parenting manual provides information that can improve our parenting skills, thus promoting positive behavior in our children and adults. In this human race there is always going to be room for improvement. Nevertheless, we must turn to the truth. We must be practical, conscientious, deliberate, and concise in our way of thinking and in our behavior. The way in which we methodically live our lives clearly is not the lifestyle in which Christ planned for us to live; our way is detrimental to us. Now is the time to arrest the detriments we're imposing on ourselves as a human race. We mimic each other's mistakes even though there are specific plans written for us to live by.

We do have a savior to light our way!

Acts 4:12 says, "Neither is there salvation in any other: for there is none other name under heaven given among men, whereby we must be saved."

For example, read Matthew 19:18–20. "He saith unto him, Which? Jesus said, Thou shalt do no murder, Thou shalt not commit adultery, Thou shalt not steal, Thou shalt not bear false witness, Honour thy father and *thy* mother: and, Thou shalt love thy neighbour as thyself. The young man saith unto him, All these things have I kept from my youth up: what lack I yet?"

Matthew 6:9 says, "After this manner therefore pray ye: Our Father which art in heaven, Hallowed be thy name."

Matthew 12:25 says, "The young man saith unto him, All these things have I kept from my youth up: what lack I yet?"

Hebrews 10:31 says, "*It is* a fearful thing to fall into the hands of the living God."

Hebrews 11:6 says, "But without faith *it is* impossible to please *him*: for he that cometh to God must believe that he is, and *that* he is a rewarder of them that diligently seek him."

Proverbs 1:7 says, "The fear of the Lord *is* the beginning of knowledge: *but* fools despise wisdom and instruction."

Proverbs 3:5–6 says, "Trust in the Lord with all thine heart; and lean not unto thine own understanding. In all thy ways acknowledge him, and he shall direct thy paths."

Proverbs 4:5–9 says, "Get wisdom, get understanding: forget *it* not; neither decline from the words of my mouth. Forsake her not, and she shall preserve thee: love her, and she shall keep thee. Wisdom *is* the principal thing; *therefore* get wisdom: and with all thy getting get understanding. Exalt her, and she shall promote thee: she shall bring thee to honour, when thou dost embrace her. She shall give to thine head an ornament of grace: a crown of glory shall she deliver to thee."

Proverbs 6:16–19 says, "These six *things* doth the Lord hate: yea, seven *are* an abomination unto him: A proud look, a lying tongue, and hands that shed innocent blood, An heart that deviseth wicked imaginations, feet that be swift in running to mischief, A false witness *that* speaketh lies, and he that soweth discord among brethren."

Proverbs 9:10 says, "The fear of the Lord *is* the beginning of wisdom: and the knowledge of the holy *is* understanding."

Proverbs 12:2 says, "A good *man* obtaineth favour of the Lord: but a man of wicked devices will he condemn."

Proverbs 14:12, 19, 30, 33 says, "There is a way which seemeth right unto a man, but the end thereof *are* the ways of death … The lip of truth shall be established for ever: but a lying tongue *is* but for a moment … A sound heart *is* the life of the flesh: but envy the rottenness of the bones … Wisdom resteth in the heart of him that hath understanding: but *that which is* in the midst of fools is made known."

Prov. 15:2, 19, 21, 32–33 says, "The tongue of the wise useth knowledge aright: but the mouth of fools poureth out foolishness ... The way of the slothful *man is* as an hedge of thorns: but the way of the righteous *is* made plain ... Folly *is* joy to *him that is* destitute of wisdom: but a man of understanding walketh uprightly ... He that refuseth instruction despiseth his own soul: but he that heareth reproof getteth understanding. The fear of the Lord *is* the instruction of wisdom; and before honour *is* humility."

Proverbs 16:2, 7–8, 18, 25 says, "All the ways of a man *are* clean in his own eyes; but the Lord weigheth the spirits ... When a man's ways please the Lord, he maketh even his enemies to be at peace with him. Better *is* a little with righteousness than great revenues without right ... Pride *goeth* before destruction, and an haughty spirit before a fall ... There is a way that seemeth right unto a man, but the end thereof *are* the ways of death."

Proverbs 18:21, 24 says, "Death and life *are* in the power of the tongue: and they that love it shall eat the fruit thereof ... A man *that hath* friends must shew himself friendly: and there is a friend *that* sticketh closer than a brother."

Proverbs 20:1, 4, 6, 11, 15, 24 says, "Wine *is* a mocker, strong drink *is* raging: and whosoever is deceived thereby isn't wise ... The sluggard won't plow by reason of the cold; *therefore* shall he beg in harvest, and *have* nothing ... Most men will proclaim everyone his own goodness: but a faithful man who can find? ... Even a child is known by his doings, whether his work *be* pure, and whether *it be* right ... There is gold, and a multitude of rubies: but the lips of knowledge *are* a precious jewel ... Man's goings *are* of the Lord; how can a man then understand his own way?"

Proverbs 21:1–2, 8, 25 says, "The king's heart is in the hand of the Lord, as the rivers of water: he turneth it whithersoever he will. Every way of a man *is* right in his own eyes: but the Lord pondereth the hearts ... The way of man *is* froward and strange: but *as for* the pure, his work *is* right. *It is* better to dwell in a corner of the housetop, than with a brawling woman in a wide house ... The desire of the slothful killeth him; for his hands refuse to labour."

Proverbs 22:24 says, "Make no friendship with an angry man; and with a furious man thou shalt not go."

Proverbs 2:18–19 says, "A man that beareth false witness against his neighbour *is* a maul, and a sword, and a sharp arrow. Confidence in an unfaithful man in time of trouble *is like* a broken tooth, and a foot out of joint."

Proverbs 26:14 says, "*As* the door turneth upon his hinges, so *doth* the slothful upon his bed."

Proverbs 27:20 says, "Hell and destruction are never full; so the eyes of man are never satisfied."

Proverbs 28:5–6, 13, 21 says, "Evil men understand not judgment: but they that seek the Lord understand all *things*. Better *is* the poor that walketh in his uprightness, than *he that is* perverse *in his* ways, though he *be* rich ... He that covereth his sins shall not prosper: but whoso confesseth and forsaketh *them* shall have mercy ... To have respect of persons *is* not good: for for a piece of bread *that* man will transgress."

Proverbs 29:25 says, "The fear of man bringeth a snare: but whoso putteth his trust in the Lord shall be safe."

Proverbs 30:9 says, "Lest I be full, and deny *thee*, and say, Who *is* the Lord? or lest I be poor, and steal, and take the name of my God *in vain*."

Proverbs 31:3, 11–31 says,

Give not thy strength unto women, nor thy ways to that which destroyeth kings the heart of her husband doth safely trust in her, so that he shall have no need of spoil. She will do him good and not evil all the days of her life. She seeketh wool, and flax, and worketh willingly with her hands. She is like the merchants' ships; she bringeth her food from afar. She riseth also while it is yet night, and giveth meat to her household, and a portion to her maidens. She considereth a field, and buyeth it: with the fruit of her hands she planteth a vineyard. She girdeth her loins with strength, and strengtheneth her arms. She perceiveth that her merchandise is good: her candle goeth not out by night. She layeth her hands to the spindle, and her hands hold the distaff. She stretcheth out her hand to the poor; yea, she reacheth forth her hands to the needy. She is not afraid of the snow for her household: for all her household are clothed with scarlet. She maketh herself coverings of tapestry; her clothing is silk and purple. Her husband is known in the gates, when he sitteth among the elders of the land. She maketh fine linen, and selleth it; and delivereth girdles unto the merchant. Strength and honour are her clothing; and she shall rejoice in time to come. She openeth her mouth with wisdom; and in her tongue is the law of kindness. She looketh well to the ways of her household, and eateth not the bread of idleness. Her children arise up, and call her blessed; her husband also, and he praiseth her. Many daughters have done virtuously, but thou excellest them all. Favour is deceitful, and beauty is vain: but a woman that feareth the Lord, she shall be praised. Give her of the fruit of her hands; and let her own works praise her in the gates.

Matthew 6:9–13 says, "After this manner therefore pray ye: Our Father which art in heaven, Hallowed be thy name. Thy kingdom come. Thy will be done in earth, as *it is* in heaven. Give us this day our daily bread. And forgive us our debts, as we forgive our debtors. And lead us not into temptation, but deliver us from evil: For thine is the kingdom, and the power, and the glory, forever. Amen."

Matthew 12:25 says, "And Jesus knew their thoughts, and said unto them, Every kingdom divided against itself is brought to desolation; and every city or house divided against itself shall not stand."

Matthew 19:18–20 says, "He saith unto him, Which? Jesus said, Thou shalt do no murder, Thou shalt not commit adultery, Thou shalt not steal, Thou shalt not bear false witness, Honour thy father and *thy* mother: and, Thou shalt love thy neighbour as thyself. The young man saith unto him, All these things have I kept from my youth up: what lack I yet?"

Ephesians 5:22 says, "Wives, submit yourselves unto your own husbands, as unto the Lord."

Hebrews 10:31 says, "*It is* a fearful thing to fall into the hands of the living God."

Hebrews 11:6 says, "But without faith *it is* impossible to please *him:* for he that cometh to God must believe that he is, and *that* he is a rewarder of them that diligently seek him."

Acts 4:12 says, "Neither is there salvation in any other: for there is none other name under heaven given among men, whereby we must be saved."

Parenting

is as

Important

and as

Methodical

as that!

APPENDIX

THE KING JAMES VERSION OF THE BOOK OF PROVERBS

Proverbs Chapter 1

1   The proverbs of Solomon the son of David, king of Israel;

2   To know wisdom and instruction; to perceive the words of understanding;

3   To receive the instruction of wisdom, justice, and judgment, and equity;

4   To give subtilty to the simple, to the young man knowledge and discretion.

5   A wise *man* will hear, and will increase learning; and a man of understanding shall attain unto wise counsels:

6   To understand a proverb, and the interpretation; the words of the wise, and their dark sayings.

⁷ The fear of the LORD *is* the beginning of knowledge: *but* fools despise wisdom and instruction.

⁸ My son, hear the instruction of thy father, and forsake not the law of thy mother:

⁹ For they *shall be* an ornament of grace unto thy head, and chains about thy neck.

¹⁰ My son, if sinners entice thee, consent thou not.

¹¹ If they say, Come with us, let us lay wait for blood, let us lurk privily for the innocent without cause:

¹² Let us swallow them up alive as the grave; and whole, as those that go down into the pit:

¹³ We shall find all precious substance, we shall fill our houses with spoil:

¹⁴ Cast in thy lot among us; let us all have one purse:

¹⁵ My son, walk not thou in the way with them; refrain thy foot from their path:

¹⁶ For their feet run to evil, and make haste to shed blood.

¹⁷ Surely in vain the net is spread in the sight of any bird.

¹⁸ And they lay wait for their *own* blood; they lurk privily for their *own* lives.

¹⁹ So *are* the ways of every one that is greedy of gain; *which* taketh away the life of the owners thereof.

²⁰ Wisdom crieth without; she uttereth her voice in the streets:

²¹ She crieth in the chief place of concourse, in the openings of the gates: in the city she uttereth her words, *saying,*

²² How long, ye simple ones, will ye love simplicity? and the scorners delight in their scorning, and fools hate knowledge?

²³ Turn you at my reproof: behold, I will pour out my spirit unto you, I will make known my words unto you.

²⁴ Because I have called, and ye refused; I have stretched out my hand, and no man regarded;

²⁵ But ye have set at nought all my counsel, and would none of my reproof:

²⁶ I also will laugh at your calamity; I will mock when your fear cometh;

²⁷ When your fear cometh as desolation, and your destruction cometh as a whirlwind; when distress and anguish cometh upon you.

²⁸ Then shall they call upon me, but I will not answer; they shall seek me early, but they shall not find me:

²⁹ For that they hated knowledge, and did not choose the fear of the LORD:

³⁰ They would none of my counsel: they despised all my reproof.

³¹ Therefore shall they eat of the fruit of their own way, and be filled with their own devices.

³² For the turning away of the simple shall slay them, and the prosperity of fools shall destroy them.

³³ But whoso hearkeneth unto me shall dwell safely, and shall be quiet from fear of evil.

Proverbs Chapter 2

1 My son, if thou wilt receive my words, and hide my commandments with thee;

2 So that thou incline thine ear unto wisdom, *and* apply thine heart to understanding;

3 Yea, if thou criest after knowledge, *and* liftest up thy voice for understanding;

4 If thou seekest her as silver, and searchest for her as *for* hid treasures;

5 Then shalt thou understand the fear of the LORD, and find the knowledge of God.

6 For the LORD giveth wisdom: out of his mouth *cometh* knowledge and understanding.

7 He layeth up sound wisdom for the righteous: *he is* a buckler to them that walk uprightly.

8 He keepeth the paths of judgment, and preserveth the way of his saints.

9 Then shalt thou understand righteousness, and judgment, and equity; *yea*, every good path.

10 When wisdom entereth into thine heart, and knowledge is pleasant unto thy soul;

11 Discretion shall preserve thee, understanding shall keep thee:

12 To deliver thee from the way of the evil *man*, from the man that speaketh froward things;

13 Who leave the paths of uprightness, to walk in the ways of darkness;

¹⁴ Who rejoice to do evil, *and* delight in the frowardness of the wicked;

¹⁵ Whose ways *are* crooked, and *they* froward in their paths:

¹⁶ To deliver thee from the strange woman, *even* from the stranger *which* flattereth with her words;

¹⁷ Which forsaketh the guide of her youth, and forgetteth the covenant of her God.

¹⁸ For her house inclineth unto death, and her paths unto the dead.

¹⁹ None that go unto her return again, neither take they hold of the paths of life.

²⁰ That thou mayest walk in the way of good *men*, and keep the paths of the righteous.

²¹ For the upright shall dwell in the land, and the perfect shall remain in it.

²² But the wicked shall be cut off from the earth, and the transgressors shall be rooted out of it.

Proverbs Chapter 2

¹ My son, forget not my law; but let thine heart keep my commandments:

² For length of days, and long life, and peace, shall they add to thee.

³ Let not mercy and truth forsake thee: bind them about thy neck; write them upon the table of thine heart:

4 So shalt thou find favour and good understanding in the sight of God and man.

5 Trust in the LORD with all thine heart; and lean not unto thine own understanding.

6 In all thy ways acknowledge him, and he shall direct thy paths.

7 Be not wise in thine own eyes: fear the LORD, and depart from evil.

8 It shall be health to thy navel, and marrow to thy bones.

9 Honour the LORD with thy substance, and with the firstfruits of all thine increase:

10 So shall thy barns be filled with plenty, and thy presses shall burst out with new wine.

11 My son, despise not the chastening of the LORD; neither be weary of his correction:

12 For whom the LORD loveth he correcteth; even as a father the son *in whom* he delighteth.

13 Happy *is* the man *that* findeth wisdom, and the man *that* getteth understanding.

14 For the merchandise of it *is* better than the merchandise of silver, and the gain thereof than fine gold.

15 She *is* more precious than rubies: and all the things thou canst desire are not to be compared unto her.

16 Length of days *is* in her right hand; *and* in her left hand riches and honour.

¹⁷ Her ways *are* ways of pleasantness, and all her paths *are* peace.

¹⁸ She *is* a tree of life to them that lay hold upon her: and happy *is every one* that retaineth her.

¹⁹ The LORD by wisdom hath founded the earth; by understanding hath he established the heavens.

²⁰ By his knowledge the depths are broken up, and the clouds drop down the dew.

²¹ My son, let not them depart from thine eyes: keep sound wisdom and discretion:

²² So shall they be life unto thy soul, and grace to thy neck.

²³ Then shalt thou walk in thy way safely, and thy foot shall not stumble.

²⁴ When thou liest down, thou shalt not be afraid: yea, thou shalt lie down, and thy sleep shall be sweet.

²⁵ Be not afraid of sudden fear, neither of the desolation of the wicked, when it cometh.

²⁶ For the LORD shall be thy confidence, and shall keep thy foot from being taken.

²⁷ Withhold not good from them to whom it is due, when it is in the power of thine hand to do *it*.

²⁸ Say not unto thy neighbour, Go, and come again, and to morrow I will give; when thou hast it by thee.

²⁹ Devise not evil against thy neighbour, seeing he dwelleth securely by thee.

30 Strive not with a man without cause, if he have done thee no harm.

31 Envy thou not the oppressor, and choose none of his ways.

32 For the froward *is* abomination to the LORD: but his secret *is* with the righteous.

33 The curse of the LORD *is* in the house of the wicked: but he blesseth the habitation of the just.

34 Surely he scorneth the scorners: but he giveth grace unto the lowly.

35 The wise shall inherit glory: but shame shall be the promotion of fools.

Proverbs Chapter 4

1 Hear, ye children, the instruction of a father, and attend to know understanding.

2 For I give you good doctrine, forsake ye not my law.

3 For I was my father's son, tender and only *beloved* in the sight of my mother.

4 He taught me also, and said unto me, Let thine heart retain my words: keep my commandments, and live.

5 Get wisdom, get understanding: forget *it* not; neither decline from the words of my mouth.

6 Forsake her not, and she shall preserve thee: love her, and she shall keep thee.

7 Wisdom *is* the principal thing; *therefore* get wisdom: and with all thy getting get understanding.

8 Exalt her, and she shall promote thee: she shall bring thee to honour, when thou dost embrace her.

9 She shall give to thine head an ornament of grace: a crown of glory shall she deliver to thee.

10 Hear, O my son, and receive my sayings; and the years of thy life shall be many.

11 I have taught thee in the way of wisdom; I have led thee in right paths.

12 When thou goest, thy steps shall not be straitened; and when thou runnest, thou shalt not stumble.

13 Take fast hold of instruction; let *her* not go: keep her; for she *is* thy life.

14 Enter not into the path of the wicked, and go not in the way of evil *men*.

15 Avoid it, pass not by it, turn from it, and pass away.

16 For they sleep not, except they have done mischief; and their sleep is taken away, unless they cause *some* to fall.

17 For they eat the bread of wickedness, and drink the wine of violence.

18 But the path of the just *is* as the shining light, that shineth more and more unto the perfect day.

19 The way of the wicked *is* as darkness: they know not at what they stumble.

20 My son, attend to my words; incline thine ear unto my sayings.

21 Let them not depart from thine eyes; keep them in the midst of thine heart.

22 For they *are* life unto those that find them, and health to all their flesh.

23 Keep thy heart with all diligence; for out of it *are* the issues of life.

24 Put away from thee a froward mouth, and perverse lips put far from thee.

25 Let thine eyes look right on, and let thine eyelids look straight before thee.

26 Ponder the path of thy feet, and let all thy ways be established.

27 Turn not to the right hand nor to the left: remove thy foot from evil.

Proverbs Chapter 5

1 My son, attend unto my wisdom, *and* bow thine ear to my understanding:

2 That thou mayest regard discretion, and *that* thy lips may keep knowledge.

3 For the lips of a strange woman drop *as* an honeycomb, and her mouth *is* smoother than oil:

4 But her end is bitter as wormwood, sharp as a twoedged sword.

5 Her feet go down to death; her steps take hold on hell.

6 Lest thou shouldest ponder the path of life, her ways are moveable, *that* thou canst not know *them*.

7 Hear me now therefore, O ye children, and depart not from the words of my mouth.

8 Remove thy way far from her, and come not nigh the door of her house:

9 Lest thou give thine honour unto others, and thy years unto the cruel:

10 Lest strangers be filled with thy wealth; and thy labours *be* in the house of a stranger;

11 And thou mourn at the last, when thy flesh and thy body are consumed,

12 And say, How have I hated instruction, and my heart despised reproof;

13 And have not obeyed the voice of my teachers, nor inclined mine ear to them that instructed me!

14 I was almost in all evil in the midst of the congregation and assembly.

15 Drink waters out of thine own cistern, and running waters out of thine own well.

16 Let thy fountains be dispersed abroad, *and* rivers of waters in the streets.

17 Let them be only thine own, and not strangers' with thee.

18 Let thy fountain be blessed: and rejoice with the wife of thy youth.

¹⁹ *Let her be as* the loving hind and pleasant roe; let her breasts satisfy thee at all times; and be thou ravished always with her love.

²⁰ And why wilt thou, my son, be ravished with a strange woman, and embrace the bosom of a stranger?

²¹ For the ways of man *are* before the eyes of the LORD, and he pondereth all his goings.

²² His own iniquities shall take the wicked himself, and he shall be holden with the cords of his sins.

²³ He shall die without instruction; and in the greatness of his folly he shall go astray.

Proverbs Chapter 6

¹ My son, if thou be surety for thy friend, *if* thou hast stricken thy hand with a stranger,

² Thou art snared with the words of thy mouth, thou art taken with the words of thy mouth.

³ Do this now, my son, and deliver thyself, when thou art come into the hand of thy friend; go, humble thyself, and make sure thy friend.

⁴ Give not sleep to thine eyes, nor slumber to thine eyelids.

⁵ Deliver thyself as a roe from the hand *of the hunter,* and as a bird from the hand of the fowler.

⁶ Go to the ant, thou sluggard; consider her ways, and be wise:

7 Which having no guide, overseer, or ruler,

8 Provideth her meat in the summer, *and* gathereth her food in the harvest.

9 How long wilt thou sleep, O sluggard? when wilt thou arise out of thy sleep?

10 *Yet* a little sleep, a little slumber, a little folding of the hands to sleep:

11 So shall thy poverty come as one that travelleth, and thy want as an armed man.

12 A naughty person, a wicked man, walketh with a froward mouth.

13 He winketh with his eyes, he speaketh with his feet, he teacheth with his fingers;

14 Therefore shall his calamity come suddenly; suddenly shall he be broken without remedy.

15 These six *things* doth the LORD hate: yea, seven *are* an abomination unto him:

16 A proud look, a lying tongue, and hands that shed innocent blood,

17 An heart that deviseth wicked imaginations, feet that be swift in running to mischief,

18 A false witness *that* speaketh lies, and he that soweth discord among brethren.

19 My son, keep thy father's commandment, and forsake not the law of thy mother:

20 Bind them continually upon thine heart, *and* tie them about thy neck.

21 When thou goest, it shall lead thee; when thou sleepest, it shall keep thee; and *when* thou awakest, it shall talk with thee.

22 For the commandment *is* a lamp; and the law *is* light; and reproofs of instruction *are* the way of life:

23 To keep thee from the evil woman, from the flattery of the tongue of a strange woman.

24 Lust not after her beauty in thine heart; neither let her take thee with her eyelids.

25 For by means of a whorish woman *a man is brought* to a piece of bread: and the adulteress will hunt for the precious life.

26 Can a man take fire in his bosom, and his clothes not be burned?

27 Can one go upon hot coals, and his feet not be burned?

28 So he that goeth in to his neighbour's wife; whosoever toucheth her shall not be innocent.

29 *Men* do not despise a thief, if he steal to satisfy his soul when he is hungry;

30 But *if* he be found, he shall restore sevenfold; he shall give all the substance of his house.

31 *But* whoso committeth adultery with a woman lacketh understanding: he *that* doeth it destroyeth his own soul.

32 A wound and dishonour shall he get; and his reproach shall not be wiped away.

³³ For jealousy *is* the rage of a man: therefore he will not spare in the day of vengeance.

³⁴ He will not regard any ransom; neither will he rest content, though thou givest many gifts.

Proverbs Chapter 7

¹ My son, keep my words, and lay up my commandments with thee.

² Keep my commandments, and live; and my law as the apple of thine eye.

³ Bind them upon thy fingers, write them upon the table of thine heart.

⁴ Say unto wisdom, Thou *art* my sister; and call understanding *thy* kinswoman:

⁵ That they may keep thee from the strange woman, from the stranger *which* flattereth with her words.

⁶ For at the window of my house I looked through my casement,

⁷ And beheld among the simple ones, I discerned among the youths, a young man void of understanding,

⁸ Passing through the street near her corner; and he went the way to her house,

⁹ In the twilight, in the evening, in the black and dark night:

¹⁰ And, behold, there met him a woman *with* the attire of an harlot, and subtil of heart.

11 (She *is* loud and stubborn; her feet abide not in her house:

12 Now *is she* without, now in the streets, and lieth in wait at every corner.)

13 So she caught him, and kissed him, *and* with an impudent face said unto him,

14 *I have* peace offerings with me; this day have I payed my vows.

15 Therefore came I forth to meet thee, diligently to seek thy face, and I have found thee.

16 I have decked my bed with coverings of tapestry, with carved *works*, with fine linen of Egypt.

17 I have perfumed my bed with myrrh, aloes, and cinnamon.

18 Come, let us take our fill of love until the morning: let us solace ourselves with loves.

19 For the goodman *is* not at home, he is gone a long journey:

20 He hath taken a bag of money with him, *and* will come home at the day appointed.

21 With her much fair speech she caused him to yield, with the flattering of her lips she forced him.

22 He goeth after her straightway, as an ox goeth to the slaughter, or as a fool to the correction of the stocks;

23 Till a dart strike through his liver; as a bird hasteth to the snare, and knoweth not that it *is* for his life.

²⁴ Hearken unto me now therefore, O ye children, and attend to the words of my mouth.

²⁵ Let not thine heart decline to her ways, go not astray in her paths.

²⁶ For she hath cast down many wounded: yea, many strong *men* have been slain by her.

²⁷ Her house *is* the way to hell, going down to the chambers of death.

Proverbs Chapter 8

¹ Doth not wisdom cry? and understanding put forth her voice?

² She standeth in the top of high places, by the way in the places of the paths.

³ She crieth at the gates, at the entry of the city, at the coming in at the doors.

⁴ Unto you, O men, I call; and my voice *is* to the sons of man.

⁵ O ye simple, understand wisdom: and, ye fools, be ye of an understanding heart.

⁶ Hear; for I will speak of excellent things; and the opening of my lips *shall be* right things.

⁷ For my mouth shall speak truth; and wickedness *is* an abomination to my lips.

⁸ All the words of my mouth *are* in righteousness; *there is* nothing froward or perverse in them.

9   They *are* all plain to him that understandeth, and right to them that find knowledge.

10 Receive my instruction, and not silver; and knowledge rather than choice gold.

11 For wisdom *is* better than rubies; and all the things that may be desired are not to be compared to it.

12 I wisdom dwell with prudence, and find out knowledge of witty inventions.

13 The fear of the LORD *is* to hate evil: pride, and arrogancy, and the evil way, and the froward mouth, do I hate.

14 Counsel *is* mine, and sound wisdom: I *am* understanding; I have strength.

15 By me kings reign, and princes decree justice.

16 By me princes rule, and nobles, *even* all the judges of the earth.

17 I love them that love me; and those that seek me early shall find me.

18 Riches and honour *are* with me; *yea*, durable riches and righteousness.

19 My fruit *is* better than gold, yea, than fine gold; and my revenue than choice silver.

20 I lead in the way of righteousness, in the midst of the paths of judgment:

21 That I may cause those that love me to inherit substance; and I will fill their treasures.

22 The LORD possessed me in the beginning of his way, before his works of old.

23 I was set up from everlasting, from the beginning, or ever the earth was.

24 When *there were* no depths, I was brought forth; when *there were* no fountains abounding with water.

25 Before the mountains were settled, before the hills was I brought forth:

26 While as yet he had not made the earth, nor the fields, nor the highest part of the dust of the world.

27 When he prepared the heavens, I *was* there: when he set a compass upon the face of the depth:

28 When he established the clouds above: when he strengthened the fountains of the deep:

29 When he gave to the sea his decree, that the waters should not pass his commandment: when he appointed the foundations of the earth:

30 Then I was by him, *as* one brought up *with him*: and I was daily *his* delight, rejoicing always before him;

31 Rejoicing in the habitable part of his earth; and my delights *were* with the sons of men.

32 Now therefore hearken unto me, O ye children: for blessed *are they that* keep my ways.

33 Hear instruction, and be wise, and refuse it not.

34 Blessed *is* the man that heareth me, watching daily at my gates, waiting at the posts of my doors.

35 For whoso findeth me findeth life, and shall obtain favour of the LORD.

36 But he that sinneth against me wrongeth his own soul: all they that hate me love death.

1   Wisdom hath builded her house, she hath hewn out her seven pillars:

2   She hath killed her beasts; she hath mingled her wine; she hath also furnished her table.

3   She hath sent forth her maidens: she crieth upon the highest places of the city,

4   Whoso *is* simple, let him turn in hither: *as for* him that wanteth understanding, she saith to him,

5   Come, eat of my bread, and drink of the wine *which* I have mingled.

6   Forsake the foolish, and live; and go in the way of understanding.

7   He that reproveth a scorner getteth to himself shame: and he that rebuketh a wicked *man getteth* himself a blot.

8   Reprove not a scorner, lest he hate thee: rebuke a wise man, and he will love thee.

9   Give *instruction* to a wise *man*, and he will be yet wiser: teach a just *man*, and he will increase in learning.

10 The fear of the LORD *is* the beginning of wisdom: and the knowledge of the holy *is* understanding.

11 For by me thy days shall be multiplied, and the years of thy life shall be increased.

12 If thou be wise, thou shalt be wise for thyself: but *if* thou scornest, thou alone shalt bear *it*.

¹³ A foolish woman *is* clamorous: *she is* simple, and knoweth nothing.

¹⁴ For she sitteth at the door of her house, on a seat in the high places of the city,

¹⁵ To call passengers who go right on their ways:

¹⁶ Whoso *is* simple, let him turn in hither: and *as for* him that wanteth understanding, she saith to him,

¹⁷ Stolen waters are sweet, and bread *eaten* in secret is pleasant.

¹⁸ But he knoweth not that the dead *are* there; *and that* her guests *are* in the depths of hell.

Proverbs Chapter 10

¹ The proverbs of Solomon. A wise son maketh a glad father: but a foolish son *is* the heaviness of his mother.

² Treasures of wickedness profit nothing: but righteousness delivereth from death.

³ The LORD will not suffer the soul of the righteous to famish: but he casteth away the substance of the wicked.

⁴ He becometh poor that dealeth *with* a slack hand: but the hand of the diligent maketh rich.

⁵ He that gathereth in summer *is* a wise son: *but* he that sleepeth in harvest *is* a son that causeth shame.

⁶ Blessings *are* upon the head of the just: but violence covereth the mouth of the wicked.

7 The memory of the just *is* blessed: but the name of the wicked shall rot.

8 The wise in heart will receive commandments: but a prating fool shall fall.

9 He that walketh uprightly walketh surely: but he that perverteth his ways shall be known.

10 He that winketh with the eye causeth sorrow: but a prating fool shall fall.

11 The mouth of a righteous *man is* a well of life: but violence covereth the mouth of the wicked.

12 Hatred stirreth up strifes: but love covereth all sins.

13 In the lips of him that hath understanding wisdom is found: but a rod *is* for the back of him that is void of understanding.

14 Wise *men* lay up knowledge: but the mouth of the foolish *is* near destruction.

15 The rich man's wealth *is* his strong city: the destruction of the poor *is* their poverty.

16 The labour of the righteous *tendeth* to life: the fruit of the wicked to sin.

17 He *is in* the way of life that keepeth instruction: but he that refuseth reproof erreth.

18 He that hideth hatred *with* lying lips, and he that uttereth a slander, *is* a fool.

19 In the multitude of words there wanteth not sin: but he that refraineth his lips *is* wise.

20 The tongue of the just *is as* choice silver: the heart of the wicked *is* little worth.

21 The lips of the righteous feed many: but fools die for want of wisdom.

22 The blessing of the LORD, it maketh rich, and he addeth no sorrow with it.

23 *It is* as sport to a fool to do mischief: but a man of understanding hath wisdom.

24 The fear of the wicked, it shall come upon him: but the desire of the righteous shall be granted.

25 As the whirlwind passeth, so *is* the wicked no *more*: but the righteous *is* an everlasting foundation.

26 As vinegar to the teeth, and as smoke to the eyes, so *is* the sluggard to them that send him.

27 The fear of the LORD prolongeth days: but the years of the wicked shall be shortened.

28 The hope of the righteous *shall be* gladness: but the expectation of the wicked shall perish.

29 The way of the LORD *is* strength to the upright: but destruction *shall be* to the workers of iniquity.

30 The righteous shall never be removed: but the wicked shall not inhabit the earth.

31 The mouth of the just bringeth forth wisdom: but the froward tongue shall be cut out.

32 The lips of the righteous know what is acceptable: but the mouth of the wicked *speaketh* frowardness.

Proverbs Chapter 11

¹ A false balance *is* abomination to the LORD: but a just weight *is* his delight.

² *When* pride cometh, then cometh shame: but with the lowly *is* wisdom.

³ The integrity of the upright shall guide them: but the perverseness of transgressors shall destroy them.

⁴ Riches profit not in the day of wrath: but righteousness delivereth from death.

⁵ The righteousness of the perfect shall direct his way: but the wicked shall fall by his own wickedness.

⁶ The righteousness of the upright shall deliver them: but transgressors shall be taken in *their own* naughtiness.

⁷ When a wicked man dieth, *his* expectation shall perish: and the hope of unjust *men* perisheth.

⁸ The righteous is delivered out of trouble, and the wicked cometh in his stead.

⁹ An hypocrite with *his* mouth destroyeth his neighbour: but through knowledge shall the just be delivered.

¹⁰ When it goeth well with the righteous, the city rejoiceth: and when the wicked perish, *there is* shouting.

¹¹ By the blessing of the upright the city is exalted: but it is overthrown by the mouth of the wicked.

¹² He that is void of wisdom despiseth his neighbour: but a man of understanding holdeth his peace.

13 A talebearer revealeth secrets: but he that is of a faithful spirit concealeth the matter.

14 Where no counsel *is*, the people fall: but in the multitude of counsellors *there is* safety.

15 He that is surety for a stranger shall smart *for it*: and he that hateth suretiship is sure.

16 A gracious woman retaineth honour: and strong *men* retain riches.

17 The merciful man doeth good to his own soul: but *he that is* cruel troubleth his own flesh.

18 The wicked worketh a deceitful work: but to him that soweth righteousness *shall be* a sure reward.

19 As righteousness *tendeth* to life: so he that pursueth evil *pursueth it* to his own death.

20 They that are of a froward heart *are* abomination to the LORD: but *such as are* upright in *their* way *are* his delight.

21 *Though* hand *join* in hand, the wicked shall not be unpunished: but the seed of the righteous shall be delivered.

22 *As* a jewel of gold in a swine's snout, *so is* a fair woman which is without discretion.

23 The desire of the righteous *is* only good: *but* the expectation of the wicked *is* wrath.

24 There is that scattereth, and yet increaseth; and *there is* that withholdeth more than is meet, but *it tendeth* to poverty.

25 The liberal soul shall be made fat: and he that watereth shall be watered also himself.

26 He that withholdeth corn, the people shall curse him: but blessing *shall be* upon the head of him that selleth *it*.

27 He that diligently seeketh good procureth favour: but he that seeketh mischief, it shall come unto him.

28 He that trusteth in his riches shall fall: but the righteous shall flourish as a branch.

29 He that troubleth his own house shall inherit the wind: and the fool *shall be* servant to the wise of heart.

30 The fruit of the righteous *is* a tree of life; and he that winneth souls *is* wise.

31 Behold, the righteous shall be recompensed in the earth: much more the wicked and the sinner.

Proverbs Chapter 12

1 Whoso loveth instruction loveth knowledge: but he that hateth reproof *is* brutish.

2 A good *man* obtaineth favour of the LORD: but a man of wicked devices will he condemn.

3 A man shall not be established by wickedness: but the root of the righteous shall not be moved.

4 A virtuous woman *is* a crown to her husband: but she that maketh ashamed *is* as rottenness in his bones.

5 The thoughts of the righteous *are* right: *but* the counsels of the wicked *are* deceit.

6 The words of the wicked *are* to lie in wait for blood: but the mouth of the upright shall deliver them.

7 The wicked are overthrown, and *are* not: but the house of the righteous shall stand.

8 A man shall be commended according to his wisdom: but he that is of a perverse heart shall be despised.

9 *He that is* despised, and hath a servant, *is* better than he that honoureth himself, and lacketh bread.

10 A righteous *man* regardeth the life of his beast: but the tender mercies of the wicked *are* cruel.

11 He that tilleth his land shall be satisfied with bread: but he that followeth vain *persons is* void of understanding.

12 The wicked desireth the net of evil *men*: but the root of the righteous yieldeth *fruit*.

13 The wicked is snared by the transgression of *his* lips: but the just shall come out of trouble.

14 A man shall be satisfied with good by the fruit of *his* mouth: and the recompence of a man's hands shall be rendered unto him.

15 15:The way of a fool is wright in his own eyes: but he that hearkeneth unto counsel is wise.

16 A foo's warth is presently known: but a prudent covereth shame.

¹⁷ 17. He that speaketh truth sheweth forth righteousness: but a false witness deceit.

¹⁸ 18. There is that speaketh like the piercings of a sword: but the tongue of the wise is health.

¹⁹ The lip of truth shall be established for ever: but a lying tongue is but for a moment.

²⁰ Deceit is in the heart of them that imagine evil: but to the counsellors of peace is joy.

²¹ There shall no evil happen to the just: but the wicked shall be filled with mischief

²² Lying lips are abomination to the Lord: but they that deal truly are his delight

²³ A prudent man concealeth knowledge: but the heart of fools proclaimeth foolishness.

²⁴ The hand of the diligent shall bear rule: but the slothful shall be under tribute.

²⁵ Heaviness in the heart of man maketh it stoop: but a good word maketh it glad.

²⁶ The righteous is more excellent than his neighbor: but the way of the wicked seduceth them.

²⁷ The slothful man roasteth not that which he took in hunting: but the substance of a diligent man is precious

²⁸ In the way of righteousness is life; and in the pathway thereof there is no death

Proverbs Chapter 13

1 A wise son *heareth* his father's instruction: but a scorner heareth not rebuke.

2 A man shall eat good by the fruit of *his* mouth: but the soul of the transgressors *shall eat* violence.

3 He that keepeth his mouth keepeth his life: *but* he that openeth wide his lips shall have destruction.

4 The soul of the sluggard desireth, and *hath* nothing: but the soul of the diligent shall be made fat.

5 A righteous *man* hateth lying: but a wicked *man* is loathsome, and cometh to shame.

6 Righteousness keepeth *him that is* upright in the way: but wickedness overthroweth the sinner.

7 There is that maketh himself rich, yet *hath* nothing: *there is* that maketh himself poor, yet *hath* great riches.

8 The ransom of a man's life *are* his riches: but the poor heareth not rebuke.

9 The light of the righteous rejoiceth: but the lamp of the wicked shall be put out.

10 Only by pride cometh contention: but with the well advised *is* wisdom.

11 Wealth *gotten* by vanity shall be diminished: but he that gathereth by labour shall increase.

12 Hope deferred maketh the heart sick: but *when* the desire cometh, *it is* a tree of life.

¹³ Whoso despiseth the word shall be destroyed: but he that feareth the commandment shall be rewarded.

¹⁴ The law of the wise *is* a fountain of life, to depart from the snares of death.

¹⁵ Good understanding giveth favour: but the way of transgressors *is* hard.

¹⁶ Every prudent *man* dealeth with knowledge: but a fool layeth open *his* folly.

¹⁷ A wicked messenger falleth into mischief: but a faithful ambassador *is* health.

¹⁸ Poverty and shame *shall be to* him that refuseth instruction: but he that regardeth reproof shall be honoured.

¹⁹ The desire accomplished is sweet to the soul: but *it is* abomination to fools to depart from evil.

²⁰ He that walketh with wise *men* shall be wise: but a companion of fools shall be destroyed.

²¹ Evil pursueth sinners: but to the righteous good shall be repayed.

²² A good *man* leaveth an inheritance to his children's children: and the wealth of the sinner *is* laid up for the just.

²³ Much food *is in* the tillage of the poor: but there is *that is* destroyed for want of judgment.

²⁴ He that spareth his rod hateth his son: but he that loveth him chasteneth him betimes.

25 The righteous eateth to the satisfying of his soul: but the belly of the wicked shall want.

Proverbs Chapter 14

1 1.Every wise woman buildeth her house: but the foolish plucketh it down with her hands.

2 He that walketh in his uprightness feareth the LORD: but *he that is* perverse in his ways despiseth him.

3 In the mouth of the foolish *is* a rod of pride: but the lips of the wise shall preserve them.

4 Where no oxen *are*, the crib *is* clean: but much increase *is* by the strength of the ox.

5 A faithful witness will not lie: but a false witness will utter lies.

6 A scorner seeketh wisdom, and *findeth it* not: but knowledge *is* easy unto him that understandeth.

7 Go from the presence of a foolish man, when thou perceivest not *in him* the lips of knowledge.

8 The wisdom of the prudent *is* to understand his way: but the folly of fools *is* deceit.

9 Fools make a mock at sin: but among the righteous *there is* favour.

10 The heart knoweth his own bitterness; and a stranger doth not intermeddle with his joy.

11 The house of the wicked shall be overthrown: but the tabernacle of the upright shall flourish.

12 There is a way which seemeth right unto a man, but the end thereof *are* the ways of death.

13 Even in laughter the heart is sorrowful; and the end of that mirth *is* heaviness.

14 The backslider in heart shall be filled with his own ways: and a good man *shall be satisfied* from himself.

15 The simple believeth every word: but the prudent *man* looketh well to his going.

16 A wise *man* feareth, and departeth from evil: but the fool rageth, and is confident.

17 *He that is* soon angry dealeth foolishly: and a man of wicked devices is hated.

18 The simple inherit folly: but the prudent are crowned with knowledge.

19 The evil bow before the good; and the wicked at the gates of the righteous.

20 The poor is hated even of his own neighbour: but the rich *hath* many friends.

21 He that despiseth his neighbour sinneth: but he that hath mercy on the poor, happy *is* he.

22 Do they not err that devise evil? but mercy and truth *shall be* to them that devise good.

23 In all labour there is profit: but the talk of the lips *tendeth* only to penury.

24 The crown of the wise *is* their riches: *but* the foolishness of fools *is* folly.

25 A true witness delivereth souls: but a deceitful *witness* speaketh lies.

26 In the fear of the LORD *is* strong confidence: and his children shall have a place of refuge.

27 The fear of the LORD *is* a fountain of life, to depart from the snares of death.

28 In the multitude of people *is* the king's honour: but in the want of people *is* the destruction of the prince.

29 *He that is* slow to wrath *is* of great understanding: but *he that is* hasty of spirit exalteth folly.

30 A sound heart *is* the life of the flesh: but envy the rottenness of the bones.

31 He that oppresseth the poor reproacheth his Maker: but he that honoureth him hath mercy on the poor.

32 The wicked is driven away in his wickedness: but the righteous hath hope in his death.

33 Wisdom resteth in the heart of him that hath understanding: but *that which is* in the midst of fools is made known.

34 Righteousness exalteth a nation: but sin *is* a reproach to any people.

35 The king's favour *is* toward a wise servant: but his wrath is *against* him that causeth shame.

Proverbs Chapter 15

1 A soft answer turneth away wrath: but grievous words stir up anger.

2 The tongue of the wise useth knowledge aright: but the mouth of fools poureth out foolishness.

3 The eyes of the LORD *are* in every place, beholding the evil and the good.

4 A wholesome tongue *is* a tree of life: but perverseness therein *is* a breach in the spirit.

5 A fool despiseth his father's instruction: but he that regardeth reproof is prudent.

6 In the house of the righteous *is* much treasure: but in the revenues of the wicked is trouble.

7 The lips of the wise disperse knowledge: but the heart of the foolish *doeth* not so.

8 The sacrifice of the wicked *is* an abomination to the LORD: but the prayer of the upright *is* his delight.

9 The way of the wicked *is* an abomination unto the LORD: but he loveth him that followeth after righteousness.

10 Correction *is* grievous unto him that forsaketh the way: *and* he that hateth reproof shall die.

11 Hell and destruction *are* before the LORD: how much more then the hearts of the children of men?

12 A scorner loveth not one that reproveth him: neither will he go unto the wise.

13 A merry heart maketh a cheerful countenance: but by sorrow of the heart the spirit is broken.

14 The heart of him that hath understanding seeketh knowledge: but the mouth of fools feedeth on foolishness.

15 All the days of the afflicted *are* evil: but he that is of a merry heart *hath* a continual feast.

16 Better *is* little with the fear of the LORD than great treasure and trouble therewith.

17 Better *is* a dinner of herbs where love is, than a stalled ox and hatred therewith.

18 A wrathful man stirreth up strife: but *he that is* slow to anger appeaseth strife.

19 The way of the slothful *man is* as an hedge of thorns: but the way of the righteous *is* made plain.

20 A wise son maketh a glad father: but a foolish man despiseth his mother.

21 Folly *is* joy to *him that is* destitute of wisdom: but a man of understanding walketh uprightly.

22 Without counsel purposes are disappointed: but in the multitude of counsellors they are established.

23 A man hath joy by the answer of his mouth: and a word *spoken* in due season, how good *is it*!

24 The way of life *is* above to the wise, that he may depart from hell beneath.

25 The LORD will destroy the house of the proud: but he will establish the border of the widow.

26 The thoughts of the wicked *are* an abomination to the LORD: but *the words* of the pure *are* pleasant words.

27 He that is greedy of gain troubleth his own house; but he that hateth gifts shall live.

28 The heart of the righteous studieth to answer: but the mouth of the wicked poureth out evil things.

29 The LORD *is* far from the wicked: but he heareth the prayer of the righteous.

30 The light of the eyes rejoiceth the heart: *and* a good report maketh the bones fat.

31 The ear that heareth the reproof of life abideth among the wise.

32 He that refuseth instruction despiseth his own soul: but he that heareth reproof getteth understanding.

33 The fear of the LORD *is* the instruction of wisdom; and before honour *is* humility.

Proverbs Chapter 16

1 The preparations of the heart in man, and the answer of the tongue, *is* from the LORD.

2 All the ways of a man *are* clean in his own eyes; but the LORD weigheth the spirits.

3 Commit thy works unto the LORD, and thy thoughts shall be established.

4 The LORD hath made all *things* for himself: yea, even the wicked for the day of evil.

5 Every one *that is* proud in heart *is* an abomination to the LORD: *though* hand *join* in hand, he shall not be unpunished.

6 By mercy and truth iniquity is purged: and by the fear of the LORD *men* depart from evil.

7 When a man's ways please the LORD, he maketh even his enemies to be at peace with him.

8 Better *is* a little with righteousness than great revenues without right.

9 A man's heart deviseth his way: but the LORD directeth his steps.

10 A divine sentence *is* in the lips of the king: his mouth transgresseth not in judgment.

11 A just weight and balance *are* the LORD'S: all the weights of the bag *are* his work.

12 *It is* an abomination to kings to commit wickedness: for the throne is established by righteousness.

13 Righteous lips *are* the delight of kings; and they love him that speaketh right.

14 The wrath of a king *is as* messengers of death: but a wise man will pacify it.

15 In the light of the king's countenance *is* life; and his favour *is* as a cloud of the latter rain.

16 How much better *is it* to get wisdom than gold! and to get understanding rather to be chosen than silver!

17 The highway of the upright *is* to depart from evil: he that keepeth his way preserveth his soul.

18 Pride *goeth* before destruction, and an haughty spirit before a fall.

19 Better *it is to be* of an humble spirit with the lowly, than to divide the spoil with the proud.

²⁰ He that handleth a matter wisely shall find good: and whoso trusteth in the LORD, happy *is* he.

²¹ The wise in heart shall be called prudent: and the sweetness of the lips increaseth learning.

²² Understanding *is* a wellspring of life unto him that hath it: but the instruction of fools *is* folly.

²³ The heart of the wise teacheth his mouth, and addeth learning to his lips.

²⁴ Pleasant words *are as* an honeycomb, sweet to the soul, and health to the bones.

²⁵ There is a way that seemeth right unto a man, but the end thereof *are* the ways of death.

²⁶ He that laboureth laboureth for himself; for his mouth craveth it of him.

²⁷ An ungodly man diggeth up evil: and in his lips *there is* as a burning fire.

²⁸ A froward man soweth strife: and a whisperer separateth chief friends.

²⁹ A violent man enticeth his neighbour, and leadeth him into the way *that is* not good.

³⁰ He shutteth his eyes to devise froward things: moving his lips he bringeth evil to pass.

³¹ The hoary head *is* a crown of glory, *if* it be found in the way of righteousness.

³² *He that is* slow to anger *is* better than the mighty; and he that ruleth his spirit than he that taketh a city.

³³ The lot is cast into the lap; but the whole disposing thereof *is* of the LORD.

Proverbs Chapter 17

¹ Better *is* a dry morsel, and quietness therewith, than an house full of sacrifices *with* strife.

² A wise servant shall have rule over a son that causeth shame, and shall have part of the inheritance among the brethren.

³ The fining pot *is* for silver, and the furnace for gold: but the LORD trieth the hearts.

⁴ A wicked doer giveth heed to false lips; *and* a liar giveth ear to a naughty tongue.

⁵ Whoso mocketh the poor reproacheth his Maker: *and* he that is glad at calamities shall not be unpunished.

⁶ Children's children *are* the crown of old men; and the glory of children *are* their fathers.

⁷ Excellent speech becometh not a fool: much less do lying lips a prince.

⁸ A gift *is as* a precious stone in the eyes of him that hath it: whithersoever it turneth, it prospereth.

⁹ He that covereth a transgression seeketh love; but he that repeateth a matter separateth *very* friends.

¹⁰ A reproof entereth more into a wise man than an hundred stripes into a fool.

¹¹ An evil *man* seeketh only rebellion: therefore a cruel messenger shall be sent against him.

¹² Let a bear robbed of her whelps meet a man, rather than a fool in his folly.

¹³ Whoso rewardeth evil for good, evil shall not depart from his house.

¹⁴ The beginning of strife *is as* when one letteth out water: therefore leave off contention, before it be meddled with.

¹⁵ He that justifieth the wicked, and he that condemneth the just, even they both *are* abomination to the LORD.

¹⁶ Wherefore *is there* a price in the hand of a fool to get wisdom, seeing *he hath* no heart *to it*?

¹⁷ A friend loveth at all times, and a brother is born for adversity.

¹⁸ A man void of understanding striketh hands, *and* becometh surety in the presence of his friend.

¹⁹ He loveth transgression that loveth strife: *and* he that exalteth his gate seeketh destruction.

²⁰ He that hath a froward heart findeth no good: and he that hath a perverse tongue falleth into mischief.

²¹ He that begetteth a fool *doeth it* to his sorrow: and the father of a fool hath no joy.

²² A merry heart doeth good *like* a medicine: but a broken spirit drieth the bones.

²³ A wicked *man* taketh a gift out of the bosom to pervert the ways of judgment.

24 Wisdom *is* before him that hath understanding; but the eyes of a fool *are* in the ends of the earth.

25 A foolish son *is* a grief to his father, and bitterness to her that bare him.

26 Also to punish the just *is* not good, *nor* to strike princes for equity.

27 He that hath knowledge spareth his words: *and* a man of understanding is of an excellent spirit.

28 Even a fool, when he holdeth his peace, is counted wise: *and* he that shutteth his lips *is esteemed* a man of understanding.

Proverbs Chapter 18

1 Through desire a man, having separated himself, seeketh *and* intermeddleth with all wisdom.

2 A fool hath no delight in understanding, but that his heart may discover itself.

3 When the wicked cometh, *then* cometh also contempt, and with ignominy reproach.

4 The words of a man's mouth *are as* deep waters, *and* the wellspring of wisdom *as* a flowing brook.

5 *It is* not good to accept the person of the wicked, to overthrow the righteous in judgment.

6 A fool's lips enter into contention, and his mouth calleth for strokes.

7 A fool's mouth *is* his destruction, and his lips *are* the snare of his soul.

8 The words of a talebearer *are* as wounds, and they go down into the innermost parts of the belly.

9 He also that is slothful in his work is brother to him that is a great waster.

10 The name of the LORD *is* a strong tower: the righteous runneth into it, and is safe.

11 The rich man's wealth *is* his strong city, and as an high wall in his own conceit.

12 Before destruction the heart of man is haughty, and before honour *is* humility.

13 He that answereth a matter before he heareth *it*, it *is* folly and shame unto him.

14 The spirit of a man will sustain his infirmity; but a wounded spirit who can bear?

15 The heart of the prudent getteth knowledge; and the ear of the wise seeketh knowledge.

16 A man's gift maketh room for him, and bringeth him before great men.

17 *He that is* first in his own cause *seemeth* just; but his neighbour cometh and searcheth him.

18 The lot causeth contentions to cease, and parteth between the mighty.

19 A brother offended *is harder to be won* than a strong city: and *their* contentions *are* like the bars of a castle.

20 A man's belly shall be satisfied with the fruit of his mouth; *and* with the increase of his lips shall he be filled.

21 Death and life *are* in the power of the tongue: and they that love it shall eat the fruit thereof.

22 *Whoso* findeth a wife findeth a good *thing*, and obtaineth favour of the LORD.

23 The poor useth intreaties; but the rich answereth roughly.

24 A man *that hath* friends must shew himself friendly: and there is a friend *that* sticketh closer than a brother.

Proverbs Chapter 19

1 Better *is* the poor that walketh in his integrity, than *he that is* perverse in his lips, and is a fool.

2 Also, *that* the soul *be* without knowledge, *it is* not good; and he that hasteth with *his* feet sinneth.

3 The foolishness of man perverteth his way: and his heart fretteth against the LORD.

4 Wealth maketh many friends; but the poor is separated from his neighbour.

5 A false witness shall not be unpunished, and *he that* speaketh lies shall not escape.

6 Many will intreat the favour of the prince: and every man *is* a friend to him that giveth gifts.

7 All the brethren of the poor do hate him: how much more do his friends go far from him? he pursueth *them with* words, *yet* they *are* wanting *to him*.

8 He that getteth wisdom loveth his own soul: he that keepeth understanding shall find good.

9 A false witness shall not be unpunished, and *he that* speaketh lies shall perish.

10 Delight is not seemly for a fool; much less for a servant to have rule over princes.

11 The discretion of a man deferreth his anger; and *it is* his glory to pass over a transgression.

12 The king's wrath *is* as the roaring of a lion; but his favour *is* as dew upon the grass.

13 A foolish son *is* the calamity of his father: and the contentions of a wife *are* a continual dropping.

14 House and riches *are* the inheritance of fathers: and a prudent wife *is* from the LORD.

15 Slothfulness casteth into a deep sleep; and an idle soul shall suffer hunger.

16 He that keepeth the commandment keepeth his own soul; *but* he that despiseth his ways shall die.

17 He that hath pity upon the poor lendeth unto the LORD; and that which he hath given will he pay him again.

18 Chasten thy son while there is hope, and let not thy soul spare for his crying.

19 A man of great wrath shall suffer punishment: for if thou deliver *him*, yet thou must do it again.

20 Hear counsel, and receive instruction, that thou mayest be wise in thy latter end.

21 *There are* many devices in a man's heart; nevertheless the counsel of the LORD, that shall stand.

22 The desire of a man *is* his kindness: and a poor man *is* better than a liar.

23 The fear of the LORD *tendeth* to life: and *he that hath it* shall abide satisfied; he shall not be visited with evil.

24 A slothful *man* hideth his hand in *his* bosom, and will not so much as bring it to his mouth again.

25 Smite a scorner, and the simple will beware: and reprove one that hath understanding, *and* he will understand knowledge.

26 He that wasteth *his* father, *and* chaseth away *his* mother, *is* a son that causeth shame, and bringeth reproach.

27 Cease, my son, to hear the instruction *that causeth* to err from the words of knowledge.

28 An ungodly witness scorneth judgment: and the mouth of the wicked devoureth iniquity.

29 Judgments are prepared for scorners, and stripes for the back of fools.

Proverbs Chapter 20

1 Wine *is* a mocker, strong drink *is* raging: and whosoever is deceived thereby is not wise.

2 The fear of a king *is* as the roaring of a lion: *whoso* provoketh him to anger sinneth *against* his own soul.

³ *It is* an honour for a man to cease from strife: but every fool will be meddling.

⁴ The sluggard will not plow by reason of the cold; *therefore* shall he beg in harvest, and *have* nothing.

⁵ Counsel in the heart of man *is like* deep water; but a man of understanding will draw it out.

⁶ Most men will proclaim every one his own goodness: but a faithful man who can find?

⁷ The just *man* walketh in his integrity: his children *are* blessed after him.

⁸ A king that sitteth in the throne of judgment scattereth away all evil with his eyes.

⁹ Who can say, I have made my heart clean, I am pure from my sin?

¹⁰ Divers weights, *and* divers measures, both of them *are* alike abomination to the LORD.

¹¹ Even a child is known by his doings, whether his work *be* pure, and whether *it be* right.

¹² The hearing ear, and the seeing eye, the LORD hath made even both of them.

¹³ Love not sleep, lest thou come to poverty; open thine eyes, *and* thou shalt be satisfied with bread.

¹⁴ *It is* naught, *it is* naught, saith the buyer: but when he is gone his way, then he boasteth.

¹⁵ There is gold, and a multitude of rubies: but the lips of knowledge *are* a precious jewel.

¹⁶ Take his garment that is surety *for* a stranger: and take a pledge of him for a strange woman.

¹⁷ Bread of deceit *is* sweet to a man; but afterwards his mouth shall be filled with gravel.

¹⁸ *Every* purpose is established by counsel: and with good advice make war.

¹⁹ He that goeth about *as* a talebearer revealeth secrets: therefore meddle not with him that flattereth with his lips.

²⁰ Whoso curseth his father or his mother, his lamp shall be put out in obscure darkness.

²¹ An inheritance *may be* gotten hastily at the beginning; but the end thereof shall not be blessed.

²² Say not thou, I will recompense evil; *but* wait on the LORD, and he shall save thee.

²³ Divers weights *are* an abomination unto the LORD; and a false balance *is* not good.

²⁴ Man's goings *are* of the LORD; how can a man then understand his own way?

²⁵ *It is* a snare to the man *who* devoureth *that which is* holy, and after vows to make enquiry.

²⁶ A wise king scattereth the wicked, and bringeth the wheel over them.

²⁷ The spirit of man *is* the candle of the LORD, searching all the inward parts of the belly.

²⁸ Mercy and truth preserve the king: and his throne is upholden by mercy.

²⁹ The glory of young men *is* their strength: and the beauty of old men *is* the gray head.

³⁰ The blueness of a wound cleanseth away evil: so *do* stripes the inward parts of the belly.

Proverbs Chapter 21

¹ The king's heart *is* in the hand of the LORD, *as* the rivers of water: he turneth it whithersoever he will.

² Every way of a man *is* right in his own eyes: but the LORD pondereth the hearts.

³ To do justice and judgment *is* more acceptable to the LORD than sacrifice.

⁴ An high look, and a proud heart, *and* the plowing of the wicked, *is* sin.

⁵ The thoughts of the diligent *tend* only to plenteousness; but of every one *that is* hasty only to want.

⁶ The getting of treasures by a lying tongue *is* a vanity tossed to and fro of them that seek death.

⁷ The robbery of the wicked shall destroy them; because they refuse to do judgment.

⁸ The way of man *is* froward and strange: but *as for* the pure, his work *is* right.

⁹ *It is* better to dwell in a corner of the housetop, than with a brawling woman in a wide house.

¹⁰ The soul of the wicked desireth evil: his neighbour findeth no favour in his eyes.

11 When the scorner is punished, the simple is made wise: and when the wise is instructed, he receiveth knowledge.

12 The righteous *man* wisely considereth the house of the wicked: *but God* overthroweth the wicked for *their* wickedness.

13 Whoso stoppeth his ears at the cry of the poor, he also shall cry himself, but shall not be heard.

14 A gift in secret pacifieth anger: and a reward in the bosom strong wrath.

15 *It is* joy to the just to do judgment: but destruction *shall be* to the workers of iniquity.

16 The man that wandereth out of the way of understanding shall remain in the congregation of the dead.

17 He that loveth pleasure *shall be* a poor man: he that loveth wine and oil shall not be rich.

18 The wicked *shall be* a ransom for the righteous, and the transgressor for the upright.

19 *It is* better to dwell in the wilderness, than with a contentious and an angry woman.

20 *There is* treasure to be desired and oil in the dwelling of the wise; but a foolish man spendeth it up.

21 He that followeth after righteousness and mercy findeth life, righteousness, and honour.

22 A wise *man* scaleth the city of the mighty, and casteth down the strength of the confidence thereof.

23 Whoso keepeth his mouth and his tongue keepeth his soul from troubles.

24 Proud *and* haughty scorner *is* his name, who dealeth in proud wrath.

25 The desire of the slothful killeth him; for his hands refuse to labour.

26 He coveteth greedily all the day long: but the righteous giveth and spareth not.

27 The sacrifice of the wicked *is* abomination: how much more, *when* he bringeth it with a wicked mind?

28 A false witness shall perish: but the man that heareth speaketh constantly.

29 A wicked man hardeneth his face: but *as for* the upright, he directeth his way.

30 *There is* no wisdom nor understanding nor counsel against the LORD.

31 The horse *is* prepared against the day of battle: but safety *is* of the LORD.

Proverbs Chapter 22

1 A *good* name *is* rather to be chosen than great riches, *and* loving favour rather than silver and gold.

2 The rich and poor meet together: the LORD *is* the maker of them all.

3 A prudent *man* foreseeth the evil, and hideth himself: but the simple pass on, and are punished.

4 By humility *and* the fear of the LORD *are* riches, and honour, and life.

5 Thorns *and* snares *are* in the way of the froward: he that doth keep his soul shall be far from them.

6 Train up a child in the way he should go: and when he is old, he will not depart from it.

7 The rich ruleth over the poor, and the borrower *is* servant to the lender.

8 He that soweth iniquity shall reap vanity: and the rod of his anger shall fail.

9 He that hath a bountiful eye shall be blessed; for he giveth of his bread to the poor.

10 Cast out the scorner, and contention shall go out; yea, strife and reproach shall cease.

11 He that loveth pureness of heart, *for* the grace of his lips the king *shall be* his friend.

12 The eyes of the LORD preserve knowledge, and he overthroweth the words of the transgressor.

13 The slothful *man* saith, *There is* a lion without, I shall be slain in the streets.

14 The mouth of strange women *is* a deep pit: he that is abhorred of the LORD shall fall therein.

15 Foolishness *is* bound in the heart of a child; *but* the rod of correction shall drive it far from him.

16 He that oppresseth the poor to increase his *riches, and* he that giveth to the rich, *shall* surely *come* to want.

¹⁷ Bow down thine ear, and hear the words of the wise, and apply thine heart unto my knowledge.

¹⁸ For *it is* a pleasant thing if thou keep them within thee; they shall withal be fitted in thy lips.

¹⁹ That thy trust may be in the LORD, I have made known to thee this day, even to thee.

²⁰ Have not I written to thee excellent things in counsels and knowledge,

²¹ That I might make thee know the certainty of the words of truth; that thou mightest answer the words of truth to them that send unto thee?

²² Rob not the poor, because he *is* poor: neither oppress the afflicted in the gate:

²³ For the LORD will plead their cause, and spoil the soul of those that spoiled them.

²⁴ Make no friendship with an angry man; and with a furious man thou shalt not go:

²⁵ Lest thou learn his ways, and get a snare to thy soul.

²⁶ Be not thou *one* of them that strike hands, *or* of them that are sureties for debts.

²⁷ If thou hast nothing to pay, why should he take away thy bed from under thee?

²⁸ Remove not the ancient landmark, which thy fathers have set.

²⁹ Seest thou a man diligent in his business? he shall stand before kings; he shall not stand before mean *men*.

Proverbs Chapter 23

¹ When thou sittest to eat with a ruler, consider diligently what *is* before thee:

² And put a knife to thy throat, if thou *be* a man given to appetite.

³ Be not desirous of his dainties: for they *are* deceitful meat.

⁴ Labour not to be rich: cease from thine own wisdom.

⁵ Wilt thou set thine eyes upon that which is not? for *riches* certainly make themselves wings; they fly away as an eagle toward heaven.

⁶ Eat thou not the bread of *him that hath* an evil eye, neither desire thou his dainty meats:

⁷ For as he thinketh in his heart, so *is* he: Eat and drink, saith he to thee; but his heart *is* not with thee.

⁸ The morsel *which* thou hast eaten shalt thou vomit up, and lose thy sweet words.

⁹ Speak not in the ears of a fool: for he will despise the wisdom of thy words.

¹⁰ Remove not the old landmark; and enter not into the fields of the fatherless:

¹¹ For their redeemer *is* mighty; he shall plead their cause with thee.

¹² Apply thine heart unto instruction, and thine ears to the words of knowledge.

¹³ Withhold not correction from the child: for *if* thou beatest him with the rod, he shall not die.

¹⁴ Thou shalt beat him with the rod, and shalt deliver his soul from hell.

¹⁵ My son, if thine heart be wise, my heart shall rejoice, even mine.

¹⁶ Yea, my reins shall rejoice, when thy lips speak right things.

¹⁷ Let not thine heart envy sinners: but *be thou* in the fear of the LORD all the day long.

¹⁸ For surely there is an end; and thine expectation shall not be cut off.

¹⁹ Hear thou, my son, and be wise, and guide thine heart in the way.

²⁰ Be not among winebibbers; among riotous eaters of flesh:

²¹ For the drunkard and the glutton shall come to poverty: and drowsiness shall clothe *a man* with rags.

²² Hearken unto thy father that begat thee, and despise not thy mother when she is old.

²³ Buy the truth, and sell *it* not; *also* wisdom, and instruction, and understanding.

²⁴ The father of the righteous shall greatly rejoice: and he that begetteth a wise *child* shall have joy of him.

²⁵ Thy father and thy mother shall be glad, and she that bare thee shall rejoice.

²⁶ My son, give me thine heart, and let thine eyes observe my ways.

²⁷ For a whore *is* a deep ditch; and a strange woman *is* a narrow pit.

²⁸ She also lieth in wait as *for* a prey, and increaseth the transgressors among men.

²⁹ Who hath woe? who hath sorrow? who hath contentions? who hath babbling? who hath wounds without cause? who hath redness of eyes?

³⁰ They that tarry long at the wine; they that go to seek mixed wine.

³¹ Look not thou upon the wine when it is red, when it giveth his colour in the cup, *when* it moveth itself aright.

³² At the last it biteth like a serpent, and stingeth like an adder.

³³ Thine eyes shall behold strange women, and thine heart shall utter perverse things.

³⁴ Yea, thou shalt be as he that lieth down in the midst of the sea, or as he that lieth upon the top of a mast.

³⁵ They have stricken me, *shalt thou say, and* I was not sick; they have beaten me, *and* I felt *it* not: when shall I awake? I will seek it yet again.

¹ Be not thou envious against evil men, neither desire to be with them.

² For their heart studieth destruction, and their lips talk of mischief.

³ Through wisdom is an house builded; and by understanding it is established:

⁴ And by knowledge shall the chambers be filled with all precious and pleasant riches.

⁵ A wise man *is* strong; yea, a man of knowledge increaseth strength.

⁶ For by wise counsel thou shalt make thy war: and in multitude of counsellors *there is* safety.

⁷ Wisdom *is* too high for a fool: he openeth not his mouth in the gate.

⁸ He that deviseth to do evil shall be called a mischievous person.

⁹ The thought of foolishness *is* sin: and the scorner *is* an abomination to men.

¹⁰ *If* thou faint in the day of adversity, thy strength *is* small.

¹¹ If thou forbear to deliver *them that are* drawn unto death, and *those that are* ready to be slain;

¹² If thou sayest, Behold, we knew it not; doth not he that pondereth the heart consider *it*? and he that keepeth thy soul, doth *not* he know *it*? and shall *not* he render to *every* man according to his works?

¹³ My son, eat thou honey, because *it is* good; and the honeycomb, *which is* sweet to thy taste:

¹⁴ So *shall* the knowledge of wisdom *be* unto thy soul: when thou hast found *it*, then there shall be a reward, and thy expectation shall not be cut off.

¹⁵ Lay not wait, O wicked *man*, against the dwelling of the righteous; spoil not his resting place:

¹⁶ For a just *man* falleth seven times, and riseth up again: but the wicked shall fall into mischief.

¹⁷ Rejoice not when thine enemy falleth, and let not thine heart be glad when he stumbleth:

¹⁸ Lest the LORD see *it*, and it displease him, and he turn away his wrath from him.

¹⁹ Fret not thyself because of evil *men*, neither be thou envious at the wicked;

²⁰ For there shall be no reward to the evil *man*; the candle of the wicked shall be put out.

²¹ My son, fear thou the LORD and the king: *and* meddle not with them that are given to change:

²² For their calamity shall rise suddenly; and who knoweth the ruin of them both?

²³ These *things* also *belong* to the wise. *It is* not good to have respect of persons in judgment.

²⁴ He that saith unto the wicked, Thou *art* righteous; him shall the people curse, nations shall abhor him:

²⁵ But to them that rebuke *him* shall be delight, and a good blessing shall come upon them.

26 *Every man* shall kiss *his* lips that giveth a right answer.

27 Prepare thy work without, and make it fit for thyself in the field; and afterwards build thine house.

28 Be not a witness against thy neighbour without cause; and deceive *not* with thy lips.

29 Say not, I will do so to him as he hath done to me: I will render to the man according to his work.

30 I went by the field of the slothful, and by the vineyard of the man void of understanding;

31 And, lo, it was all grown over with thorns, *and* nettles had covered the face thereof, and the stone wall thereof was broken down.

32 Then I saw, *and* considered *it* well: I looked upon *it, and* received instruction.

33 *Yet* a little sleep, a little slumber, a little folding of the hands to sleep:

34 So shall thy poverty come *as* one that travelleth; and thy want as an armed man.

Proverbs Chapter 25

1 These *are* also proverbs of Solomon, which the men of Hezekiah king of Judah copied out.

2 *It is* the glory of God to conceal a thing: but the honour of kings *is* to search out a matter.

3 The heaven for height, and the earth for depth, and the heart of kings *is* unsearchable.

⁴ Take away the dross from the silver, and there shall come forth a vessel for the finer.

⁵ Take away the wicked *from* before the king, and his throne shall be established in righteousness.

⁶ Put not forth thyself in the presence of the king, and stand not in the place of great *men*:

⁷ For better *it is* that it be said unto thee, Come up hither; than that thou shouldest be put lower in the presence of the prince whom thine eyes have seen.

⁸ Go not forth hastily to strive, lest *thou know not* what to do in the end thereof, when thy neighbour hath put thee to shame.

⁹ Debate thy cause with thy neighbour *himself*; and discover not a secret to another:

¹⁰ Lest he that heareth *it* put thee to shame, and thine infamy turn not away.

¹¹ A word fitly spoken *is like* apples of gold in pictures of silver.

¹² *As* an earring of gold, and an ornament of fine gold, *so is* a wise reprover upon an obedient ear.

¹³ As the cold of snow in the time of harvest, *so is* a faithful messenger to them that send him: for he refresheth the soul of his masters.

¹⁴ Whoso boasteth himself of a false gift *is like* clouds and wind without rain.

¹⁵ By long forbearing is a prince persuaded, and a soft tongue breaketh the bone.

16 Hast thou found honey? eat so much as is sufficient for thee, lest thou be filled therewith, and vomit it.

17 Withdraw thy foot from thy neighbour's house; lest he be weary of thee, and *so* hate thee.

18 A man that beareth false witness against his neighbour *is* a maul, and a sword, and a sharp arrow.

19 Confidence in an unfaithful man in time of trouble *is like* a broken tooth, and a foot out of joint.

20 *As* he that taketh away a garment in cold weather, *and as* vinegar upon nitre, so *is* he that singeth songs to an heavy heart.

21 If thine enemy be hungry, give him bread to eat; and if he be thirsty, give him water to drink:

22 For thou shalt heap coals of fire upon his head, and the LORD shall reward thee.

23 The north wind driveth away rain: so *doth* an angry countenance a backbiting tongue.

24 *It is* better to dwell in the corner of the housetop, than with a brawling woman and in a wide house.

25 *As* cold waters to a thirsty soul, so *is* good news from a far country.

26 A righteous man falling down before the wicked *is as* a troubled fountain, and a corrupt spring.

27 *It is* not good to eat much honey: so *for men* to search their own glory *is not* glory.

28 He that *hath* no rule over his own spirit *is like* a city *that is* broken down, *and* without walls.

Proverbs Chapter 26

1 As snow in summer, and as rain in harvest, so honour is not seemly for a fool.

2 As the bird by wandering, as the swallow by flying, so the curse causeless shall not come.

3 A whip for the horse, a bridle for the ass, and a rod for the fool's back.

4 Answer not a fool according to his folly, lest thou also be like unto him.

5 Answer a fool according to his folly, lest he be wise in his own conceit.

6 He that sendeth a message by the hand of a fool cutteth off the feet, *and* drinketh damage.

7 The legs of the lame are not equal: so *is* a parable in the mouth of fools.

8 As he that bindeth a stone in a sling, so *is* he that giveth honour to a fool.

9 *As* a thorn goeth up into the hand of a drunkard, so *is* a parable in the mouth of fools.

10 The great *God* that formed all *things* both rewardeth the fool, and rewardeth transgressors.

11 As a dog returneth to his vomit, *so* a fool returneth to his folly.

12 Seest thou a man wise in his own conceit? *there is* more hope of a fool than of him.

13 The slothful *man* saith, *There is* a lion in the way; a lion *is* in the streets.

¹⁴ *As* the door turneth upon his hinges, so *doth* the slothful upon his bed.

¹⁵ The slothful hideth his hand in *his* bosom; it grieveth him to bring it again to his mouth.

¹⁶ The sluggard *is* wiser in his own conceit than seven men that can render a reason.

¹⁷ He that passeth by, *and* meddleth with strife *belonging* not to him, *is like* one that taketh a dog by the ears.

¹⁸ As a mad *man* who casteth firebrands, arrows, and death,

¹⁹ So *is* the man *that* deceiveth his neighbour, and saith, Am not I in sport?

²⁰ Where no wood is, *there* the fire goeth out: so where *there is* no talebearer, the strife ceaseth.

²¹ *As* coals *are* to burning coals, and wood to fire; so *is* a contentious man to kindle strife.

²² The words of a talebearer *are* as wounds, and they go down into the innermost parts of the belly.

²³ Burning lips and a wicked heart *are like* a potsherd covered with silver dross.

²⁴ He that hateth dissembleth with his lips, and layeth up deceit within him;

²⁵ When he speaketh fair, believe him not: for *there are* seven abominations in his heart.

²⁶ *Whose* hatred is covered by deceit, his wickedness shall be shewed before the *whole* congregation.

²⁷ Whoso diggeth a pit shall fall therein: and he that rolleth a stone, it will return upon him.

²⁸ A lying tongue hateth *those that are* afflicted by it; and a flattering mouth worketh ruin.

Proverbs Chapter 27

¹ Boast not thyself of to morrow; for thou knowest not what a day may bring forth.

² Let another man praise thee, and not thine own mouth; a stranger, and not thine own lips.

³ A stone *is* heavy, and the sand weighty; but a fool's wrath *is* heavier than them both.

⁴ Wrath *is* cruel, and anger *is* outrageous; but who *is* able to stand before envy?

⁵ Open rebuke *is* better than secret love.

⁶ Faithful *are* the wounds of a friend; but the kisses of an enemy *are* deceitful.

⁷ The full soul loatheth an honeycomb; but to the hungry soul every bitter thing is sweet.

⁸ As a bird that wandereth from her nest, so *is* a man that wandereth from his place.

⁹ Ointment and perfume rejoice the heart: so *doth* the sweetness of a man's friend by hearty counsel.

¹⁰ Thine own friend, and thy father's friend, forsake not; neither go into thy brother's house in the day of thy calamity: *for* better *is* a neighbour *that is* near than a brother far off.

¹¹ My son, be wise, and make my heart glad, that I may answer him that reproacheth me.

¹² A prudent *man* foreseeth the evil, *and* hideth himself; *but* the simple pass on, *and* are punished.

¹³ Take his garment that is surety for a stranger, and take a pledge of him for a strange woman.

¹⁴ He that blesseth his friend with a loud voice, rising early in the morning, it shall be counted a curse to him.

¹⁵ A continual dropping in a very rainy day and a contentious woman are alike.

¹⁶ Whosoever hideth her hideth the wind, and the ointment of his right hand, *which* bewrayeth *itself.*

¹⁷ Iron sharpeneth iron; so a man sharpeneth the countenance of his friend.

¹⁸ Whoso keepeth the fig tree shall eat the fruit thereof: so he that waiteth on his master shall be honoured.

¹⁹ As in water face *answereth* to face, so the heart of man to man.

²⁰ Hell and destruction are never full; so the eyes of man are never satisfied.

²¹ *As* the fining pot for silver, and the furnace for gold; so *is* a man to his praise.

²² Though thou shouldest bray a fool in a mortar among wheat with a pestle, *yet* will not his foolishness depart from him.

²³ Be thou diligent to know the state of thy flocks, *and* look well to thy herds.

²⁴ For riches *are* not for ever: and doth the crown *endure* to every generation?

²⁵ The hay appeareth, and the tender grass sheweth itself, and herbs of the mountains are gathered.

²⁶ The lambs *are* for thy clothing, and the goats *are* the price of the field.

²⁷ And *thou shalt have* goats' milk enough for thy food, for the food of thy household, and *for* the maintenance for thy maidens.

Proverbs Chapter 28

¹ The wicked flee when no man pursueth: but the righteous are bold as a lion.

² For the transgression of a land many *are* the princes thereof: but by a man of understanding *and* knowledge the state *thereof* shall be prolonged.

³ A poor man that oppresseth the poor *is like* a sweeping rain which leaveth no food.

⁴ They that forsake the law praise the wicked: but such as keep the law contend with them.

⁵ Evil men understand not judgment: but they that seek the LORD understand all *things*.

⁶ Better *is* the poor that walketh in his uprightness, than *he that is* perverse *in his* ways, though he *be* rich.

7 Whoso keepeth the law *is* a wise son: but he that is a companion of riotous *men* shameth his father.

8 He that by usury and unjust gain increaseth his substance, he shall gather it for him that will pity the poor.

9 He that turneth away his ear from hearing the law, even his prayer *shall be* abomination.

10 Whoso causeth the righteous to go astray in an evil way, he shall fall himself into his own pit: but the upright shall have good *things* in possession.

11 The rich man *is* wise in his own conceit; but the poor that hath understanding searcheth him out.

12 When righteous *men* do rejoice, *there is* great glory: but when the wicked rise, a man is hidden.

13 He that covereth his sins shall not prosper: but whoso confesseth and forsaketh *them* shall have mercy.

14 Happy *is* the man that feareth alway: but he that hardeneth his heart shall fall into mischief.

15 *As* a roaring lion, and a ranging bear; *so is* a wicked ruler over the poor people.

16 The prince that wanteth understanding *is* also a great oppressor: *but* he that hateth covetousness shall prolong *his* days.

17 A man that doeth violence to the blood of *any* person shall flee to the pit; let no man stay him.

18 Whoso walketh uprightly shall be saved: but *he that is* perverse *in his* ways shall fall at once.

¹⁹ He that tilleth his land shall have plenty of bread: but he that followeth after vain *persons* shall have poverty enough.

²⁰ A faithful man shall abound with blessings: but he that maketh haste to be rich shall not be innocent.

²¹ To have respect of persons *is* not good: for for a piece of bread *that* man will transgress.

²² He that hasteth to be rich *hath* an evil eye, and considereth not that poverty shall come upon him.

²³ He that rebuketh a man afterwards shall find more favour than he that flattereth with the tongue.

²⁴ Whoso robbeth his father or his mother, and saith, *It is* no transgression; the same *is* the companion of a destroyer.

²⁵ He that is of a proud heart stirreth up strife: but he that putteth his trust in the LORD shall be made fat.

²⁶ He that trusteth in his own heart is a fool: but whoso walketh wisely, he shall be delivered.

²⁷ He that giveth unto the poor shall not lack: but he that hideth his eyes shall have many a curse.

²⁸ When the wicked rise, men hide themselves: but when they perish, the righteous increase.

Proverbs Chapter 29

1 He, that being often reproved hardeneth *his* neck, shall suddenly be destroyed, and that without remedy.

2 When the righteous are in authority, the people rejoice: but when the wicked beareth rule, the people mourn.

3 Whoso loveth wisdom rejoiceth his father: but he that keepeth company with harlots spendeth *his* substance.

4 The king by judgment establisheth the land: but he that receiveth gifts overthroweth it.

5 A man that flattereth his neighbour spreadeth a net for his feet.

6 In the transgression of an evil man *there is* a snare: but the righteous doth sing and rejoice.

7 The righteous considereth the cause of the poor: *but* the wicked regardeth not to know *it*.

8 Scornful men bring a city into a snare: but wise *men* turn away wrath.

9 *If* a wise man contendeth with a foolish man, whether he rage or laugh, *there is* no rest.

10 The bloodthirsty hate the upright: but the just seek his soul.

11 A fool uttereth all his mind: but a wise *man* keepeth it in till afterwards.

12 If a ruler hearken to lies, all his servants *are* wicked.

13 The poor and the deceitful man meet together: the LORD lighteneth both their eyes.

14 The king that faithfully judgeth the poor, his throne shall be established for ever.

15 The rod and reproof give wisdom: but a child left *to himself* bringeth his mother to shame.

16 When the wicked are multiplied, transgression increaseth: but the righteous shall see their fall.

17 Correct thy son, and he shall give thee rest; yea, he shall give delight unto thy soul.

18 Where *there is* no vision, the people perish: but he that keepeth the law, happy *is* he.

19 A servant will not be corrected by words: for though he understand he will not answer.

20 Seest thou a man *that is* hasty in his words? *there is* more hope of a fool than of him.

21 He that delicately bringeth up his servant from a child shall have him become *his* son at the length.

22 An angry man stirreth up strife, and a furious man aboundeth in transgression.

23 A man's pride shall bring him low: but honour shall uphold the humble in spirit.

24 Whoso is partner with a thief hateth his own soul: he heareth cursing, and bewrayeth *it* not.

25 The fear of man bringeth a snare: but whoso putteth his trust in the LORD shall be safe.

26 Many seek the ruler's favour; but *every* man's judgment *cometh* from the LORD.

²⁷ An unjust man *is* an abomination to the just: and *he that is* upright in the way *is* abomination to the wicked.

Proverbs Chapter 30

¹ The words of Agur the son of Jakeh, *even* the prophecy: the man spake unto Ithiel, even unto Ithiel and Ucal,

² Surely I *am* more brutish than *any* man, and have not the understanding of a man.

³ I neither learned wisdom, nor have the knowledge of the holy.

⁴ Who hath ascended up into heaven, or descended? who hath gathered the wind in his fists? who hath bound the waters in a garment? who hath established all the ends of the earth? what *is* his name, and what *is* his son's name, if thou canst tell?

⁵ Every word of God *is* pure: he *is* a shield unto them that put their trust in him.

⁶ Add thou not unto his words, lest he reprove thee, and thou be found a liar.

⁷ Two *things* have I required of thee; deny me *them* not before I die:

⁸ Remove far from me vanity and lies: give me neither poverty nor riches; feed me with food convenient for me:

9 Lest I be full, and deny *thee*, and say, Who *is* the LORD? or lest I be poor, and steal, and take the name of my God *in vain*.

10 Accuse not a servant unto his master, lest he curse thee, and thou be found guilty.

11 *There is* a generation *that* curseth their father, and doth not bless their mother.

12 *There is* a generation *that are* pure in their own eyes, and *yet* is not washed from their filthiness.

13 *There is* a generation, O how lofty are their eyes! and their eyelids are lifted up.

14 *There is* a generation, whose teeth *are as* swords, and their jaw teeth *as* knives, to devour the poor from off the earth, and the needy from *among* men.

15 The horseleach hath two daughters, *crying*, Give, give. There are three *things that* are never satisfied, *yea*, four *things* say not, It *is* enough:

16 The grave; and the barren womb; the earth *that* is not filled with water; and the fire *that* saith not, It *is* enough.

17 The eye *that* mocketh at *his* father, and despiseth to obey *his* mother, the ravens of the valley shall pick it out, and the young eagles shall eat it.

18 There be three *things which* are too wonderful for me, yea, four which I know not:

19 The way of an eagle in the air; the way of a serpent upon a rock; the way of a ship in the midst of the sea; and the way of a man with a maid.

²⁰ Such *is* the way of an adulterous woman; she eateth, and wipeth her mouth, and saith, I have done no wickedness.

²¹ For three *things* the earth is disquieted, and for four *which* it cannot bear:

²² For a servant when he reigneth; and a fool when he is filled with meat;

²³ For an odious *woman* when she is married; and an handmaid that is heir to her mistress.

²⁴ There be four *things which are* little upon the earth, but they *are* exceeding wise:

²⁵ The ants *are* a people not strong, yet they prepare their meat in the summer;

²⁶ The conies *are but* a feeble folk, yet make they their houses in the rocks;

²⁷ The locusts have no king, yet go they forth all of them by bands;

²⁸ The spider taketh hold with her hands, and is in kings' palaces.

²⁹ There be three *things* which go well, yea, four are comely in going:

³⁰ A lion *which is* strongest among beasts, and turneth not away for any;

³¹ A greyhound; an he goat also; and a king, against whom *there is* no rising up.

³² If thou hast done foolishly in lifting up thyself, or if thou hast thought evil, *lay* thine hand upon thy mouth.

³³ Surely the churning of milk bringeth forth butter, and the wringing of the nose bringeth forth blood: so the forcing of wrath bringeth forth strife.

Proverbs Chapter 31

¹ The words of king Lemuel, the prophecy that his mother taught him.

² What, my son? and what, the son of my womb? and what, the son of my vows?

³ Give not thy strength unto women, nor thy ways to that which destroyeth kings.

⁴ *It is* not for kings, O Lemuel, *it is* not for kings to drink wine; nor for princes strong drink:

⁵ Lest they drink, and forget the law, and pervert the judgment of any of the afflicted.

⁶ Give strong drink unto him that is ready to perish, and wine unto those that be of heavy hearts.

⁷ Let him drink, and forget his poverty, and remember his misery no more.

⁸ Open thy mouth for the dumb in the cause of all such as are appointed to destruction.

⁹ Open thy mouth, judge righteously, and plead the cause of the poor and needy.

¹⁰ Who can find a virtuous woman? for her price *is* far above rubies.

¹¹ The heart of her husband doth safely trust in her, so that he shall have no need of spoil.

¹² She will do him good and not evil all the days of her life.

¹³ She seeketh wool, and flax, and worketh willingly with her hands.

¹⁴ She is like the merchants' ships; she bringeth her food from afar.

¹⁵ She riseth also while it is yet night, and giveth meat to her household, and a portion to her maidens.

¹⁶ She considereth a field, and buyeth it: with the fruit of her hands she planteth a vineyard.

¹⁷ She girdeth her loins with strength, and strengtheneth her arms.

¹⁸ She perceiveth that her merchandise *is* good: her candle goeth not out by night.

¹⁹ She layeth her hands to the spindle, and her hands hold the distaff.

²⁰ She stretcheth out her hand to the poor; yea, she reacheth forth her hands to the needy.

²¹ She is not afraid of the snow for her household: for all her household *are* clothed with scarlet.

²² She maketh herself coverings of tapestry; her clothing *is* silk and purple.

²³ Her husband is known in the gates, when he sitteth among the elders of the land.

²⁴ She maketh fine linen, and selleth *it*; and delivereth girdles unto the merchant.

²⁵ Strength and honour *are* her clothing; and she shall rejoice in time to come.

²⁶ She openeth her mouth with wisdom; and in her tongue *is* the law of kindness.

²⁷ She looketh well to the ways of her household, and eateth not the bread of idleness.

²⁸ Her children arise up, and call her blessed; her husband *also*, and he praiseth her.

²⁹ Many daughters have done virtuously, but thou excellest them all.

³⁰ Favour *is* deceitful, and beauty *is* vain: *but* a woman *that* feareth the LORD, she shall be praised.

³¹ Give her of the fruit of her hands; and let her own works praise her in the gates.

Printed in the United States
By Bookmasters